Recent Titles in
Bibliographies and Indexes in Afro-American and African Studies

Black Theatre and Performance: A Pan-African Bibliography
John Gray, compiler

Health of Black Americans from Post Reconstruction to Integration, 1871–1960: An Annotated Bibliography of Contemporary Sources
Mitchell F. Rice and Woodrow Jones, Jr., compilers

Blacks in Film and Television: A Pan-African Bibliography of Films, Filmmakers, and Performers
John Gray, compiler

Daddy Grace: An Annotated Bibliography
Lenwood G. Davis, compiler

African Studies Thesaurus: Subject Headings for Library Users
Freda E. Otchere

Chester Himes: An Annotated Primary and Secondary Bibliography
Michel Fabre, Robert E. Skinner, and Lester Sullivan, compilers

A Bibliographical Guide to African-American Women Writers
Casper LeRoy Jordan, compiler

Invisible Wings: An Annotated Bibliography on Blacks in Aviation, 1916–1993
Betty Kaplan Gubert, compiler

The French Critical Reception of African-American Literature: From the Beginnings to 1970, An Annotated Bibliography
Michel Fabre, compiler, with the assistance of Rosa Bobia, Christina Davis, Charles Edwards O'Neill, and Jack Salzman

Zora Neale Hurston: An Annotated Bibliography and Reference Guide
Rose Parkman Davis, compiler

Roots of Afrocentric Thought: A Reference Guide to Negro Digest/Black World, 1961–1976
Clovis E. Semmes, compiler

African American Criminologists, 1970–1996: An Annotated Bibliography
Lee E. Ross, compiler

CONTEMPORARY AFRICAN AMERICAN FEMALE PLAYWRIGHTS

CONTEMPORARY AFRICAN AMERICAN FEMALE PLAYWRIGHTS

An Annotated Bibliography

DANA A. WILLIAMS

Bibliographies and Indexes in Afro-American and African Studies, Number 37

GREENWOOD PRESS
Westport, Connecticut • London

Library of Congress Cataloging-in-Publication Data

Williams, Dana A., 1972–
    Contemporary African American female playwrights : an annotated
bibliography / Dana A. Williams.
        p.   cm.—(Bibliographies and indexes in Afro-American and
African studies, ISSN 0742–6925 ; no. 37)
    Includes bibliographical references and index.
    ISBN 0–313–30132–8 (alk. paper)
    1. American drama—Afro-American authors—Bibliography.   2. Women
and literature—United States—History—20th century—Bibliography.
3. American drama—Afro-American authors—History and criticism—
Bibliography.   4. American drama—Women authors—History and
criticism—Bibliography.   5. American drama—20th century—History
and criticism—Bibliography.   6. American drama—Women authors—
Bibliography.   7. American drama—20th century—Bibliography.
8. Afro-Americans in literature—Bibliography.   I. Title.
II. Series.
Z1229.N39W55   1998
[PS338.N4]
016.812′540809287′08996073—dc21   98–17542

British Library Cataloguing in Publication Data is available.

Copyright © 1998 by Dana A. Williams

Library of Congress Catalog Card Number: 98–17542
ISBN: 0–313–30132–8
ISSN: 0742–6925

First published in 1998

Greenwood Press, 88 Post Road West, Westport, CT 06881
An imprint of Greenwood Publishing Group, Inc.

Printed in the United States of America

The paper used in this book complies with the
Permanent Paper Standard issued by the National
Information Standards Organization (Z39.48–1984).

10 9 8 7 6 5 4 3 2 1

For Papa, whose spirit still lives in us all,
and
For Tommi, who held his hand as he went over.

CONTENTS

PREFACE

Because research is a vital aspect of every serious academician's life, it only seems fitting that if one scholar can make research more bearable for and information more accessible to other scholars, one would not hesitate to do so. It is precisely this thought that I kept in mind while compiling this bibliography. The organization is simple but thorough, composite yet logical.

Section I contains the annotated entries of selected anthologies which include one or more plays by contemporary African American female playwrights. The annotations include bibliographic information for the anthologies and the titles of the dramas by contemporary African American women included in each anthology. In some instances, the total number of dramas anthologized in a single anthology has been included to show the under-representation of contemporary African American women in drama anthologies. Anthologies are listed in alphabetical order according to editors' last names. For those editors who have compiled more than one anthology, the anthologies are listed chronologically according to publication dates. In the rare instances when one editor has compiled more than one anthology in the same year, the titles of the anthology have been used to determine the order of listing.

Section II contains the annotated entries of selected general criticism that provides insight into dramas by contemporary African American female playwrights. The annotation contains bibliographic information and highlights which dramatists are featured in the respective works. Listings in this section follow the same pattern as Section I—alphabetical order according to editor or author.

Section III includes the annotated entries on individual dramatists, each of whom meets the following criteria for inclusion in the bibliography:

1. All playwrights are female and African American.
2. All playwrights are citizens of the United States or have resided in the United States for an extensive period of time.
3. All playwrights have had at least one drama published since 1959.

4. All playwrights have enough available information about the
   publication of their dramas to allow a helpful and informative entry.

In the first sub-section, I have provided bibliographic information on the
published dramas of selected playwrights. Many of the dramas have been published individually, and this publication information is given. To show the
representation of contemporary African American female playwrights, I have
listed the various other places where the dramas can be found such as journals,
magazines, and anthologies. For those dramas that were not published individually, bibliographic information for the anthology, magazine, or journal in which
it appears has been given. In addition, each drama entry includes a brief plot
summary. In this section, *CBAP* represents Bernard L. Peterson's *Contemporary
Black American Playwrights and Their Plays*, which is a helpful source guide for
production and publication information for selected playwrights.

The second sub-section includes a listing of and bibliographic information for
the individual dramatists' primary works that are related to drama. For those
dramatists who do not have relevant primary works, this section is omitted.

Following the primary works is the third sub-section which includes secondary sources concerning the individual playwrights and/or their dramas. These
works are separated into two sections: general articles and scholarly criticism. The
section of general articles includes selected articles found in popular magazines
and newspapers that are relevant to the playwrights or their plays. The section of
scholarly criticism includes a relatively exhaustive listing of critical articles from
scholarly journals, articles and chapters from books, and individual playwright
entries in literary dictionaries or reference books. All entries in both sections are
arranged in alphabetical order according to author of the critical citation. In cases
where an author has multiple citations, I have arranged them chronologically. In
those entries of books where I give no specific chapters or essays or page numbers,
pertinent references to the playwrights or their plays are widely dispersed in these
books. Thus, the reader should consult the respective book's index for specific
references. If certain sections (general articles or scholarly criticism) are omitted,
the respective secondary works for individual playwrights are nonexistent or
unavailable to date.

The appendix of the bibliography includes a list of selected magazines and
periodicals that frequently publish articles about playwrights and their plays and
a brief biographical sketch of each dramatist. The author index includes an alphabetical listing of all authors and editors of anthologies and collections cited in
Section I, of all authors and editors of books of general criticism cited in Section
II, and of all playwrights cited in Section III. The title index includes a list of all
anthologies and collections cited in Section I, of all books of general criticism
cited in Section II, and of all plays cited in Section III. The subject index allows
the user to locate specific subjects in relevant dramas.

Most of the information included here was compiled between 1995 and 1996,
with updates through 1997 where available. Thus, while I may attest to its

thoroughness, I must also concede, that, inevitably, it is not fully exhaustive due to limited availability of timely materials. Thus, any suggestions, corrections, and additions that may enhance or improve any future editions of this bibliography are welcomed and would be greatly appreciated. Please forward all correspondence to Dana A. Williams, P.O. Box 562, Tallulah, LA 71282.

ACKNOWLEDGMENTS

First and foremost, I must thank my family for their constant love and support. For my mother—my center, my sun; my father—from whom I get my ambition; and my sisters—my joys, I am eternally grateful. To Big John and Lin, thanks for tolerating me and for letting me turn your basement into "Bibliography Central." I must also thank Terence, whose radiance and spirit sustained me during the initial stages of this project.

Academically, I am indebted to the entire Department of English at Howard University. Since there are no words to describe the graduate faculty, I must settle for remarkable. Special thanks to Dr. R. Victoria Arana, my scholarly inspiration; Dr. Sandra G. Shannon, whose interests in drama initially motivated this project; Dr. Jeanne-Marie Miller, a leading scholar in the area of African American drama; Dr. Jennifer Jordan, whose thoroughness and organization shape this work; and Dr. John M. Reilly, whose selflessness makes every academic endeavor more bearable. I am also indebted to my academic base—the English Department at Grambling State University, particularly Dr. Anne S. Williams, who has been and always will be my academic foundation.

Near the end of this project, the world lost one of its greatest advocates of education, my maternal grandfather, my "Papa." Though he had a limited formal education, he always knew the importance of and the power in educating others. Through his children, my mother and my aunts and uncles, he helped to inform the world. In so many ways, his dedication to making knowledge more accessible to others inspired me to complete this project with pleasure. Through the family he has left behind, he continues to help, to inform and to educate the world.

INTRODUCTION

Not until 1986 when Margaret Wilkerson compiled *Nine Plays by Black Women* was there a published collection of plays exclusively by black women. As Sydné Mahone notes in her anthology *Moon Marked and Touched by Sun: Plays by African-American Women*, "the tradition of African-American women playwrights can be traced back as far as the late nineteenth century; nevertheless, contemporary women playwrights remain on the edge, scrawling in the margins of today's mainstream theater" (xiii). Even though Lorraine Hansberry's *A Raisin in the Sun* (1959) raised the world's consciousness about the abilities of African American female playwrights, both the theater and the literary world often have neglected to include African American women dramatists within the circle of production, publication, and criticism. In African American drama anthologies, female playwrights are seldom given the degree of attention that is given to male playwrights. In the *Black Drama Anthology* edited by Woodie King, Jr. and Ron Milner, of the twenty-three (23) dramas anthologized, only two, Martie Charles' *Black Cycle* and Elaine Jackson's *Toe Jam*, are authored by women. Because anthologies that exclusively collect dramas by women have limited space and are few in number, many published female playwrights go unnoticed, unread, and unproduced for reasons ranging from the work's inherent shortcomings to the playwright's failure to promote a work extensively to discrimination by a male-dominated theater world. Mahone contends that "Black women playwrights are not included in mainstream American theater because their work in some ways challenges or simply does not reflect the images and interest of the financially dominant culture, the white patriarchy. The black female playwright presents an alternative viewpoint and therefore is more likely to be embraced in those venues that serve alternative, progressive artistic agendas" (xiii). Ultimately, African American female playwrights are pushed to the margins of both American theater and the male-dominated, African American theater. But as *bell hooks* notes in *from margin to center*, "the margin need not be defined as a place that holds markings of less value; rather for African Americans, it is a 'site of resistance' to racial and gender oppression, silence, despair and invisibility" (qtd. in Mahone xiii).

In January 1990, *Time* magazine, in its "Best of the Decade" issue, selected ten dramas as the most outstanding theatrical plays of the 1980s. Of the ten dramas selected, not one was authored by a female playwright. With August Wilson being the exception, each of the others was authored by white males. Arguably, Wilson has gained full acceptance into the theatre world, becoming one of the few contemporary dramatists to have each of his published plays appear on Broadway. As noted by drama scholar Elizabeth Brown-Guillory, traditionally, the American theatre has excluded women, particularly black women: "it is because of their dogged determination to have their voices heard that these black women dramatists have been able to carve an indelible place for themselves on the American stage" (25). Despite being relegated to the margins, female playwrights like Ntozake Shange, who has published and produced over ten theater pieces, but is primarily recognized for *for colored girls who have considered suicide/when the rainbow is enuf*, and Adrienne Kennedy, whose dramas rigorously challenge reality, continue to produce artistically sound dramas that contribute tremendously to the overall production of well-crafted and meaningful American theater.

Since my principal concern while compiling this bibliography was to bring some much needed attention to contemporary female playwrights, my most challenging task was to define my scope and area of focus. Immediately, Lorraine Hansberry came to mind as the logical playwright with whom to begin. However, I did not choose to begin with Hansberry simply for logistical reasons or solely because of her popularity. I chose Hansberry because she was the first African American woman to have a drama produced on Broadway, because she was the first African American and the youngest ever playwright to receive the coveted New York Drama Critics Circle Award, and because her work has been translated into more than thirty languages and well received in over thirty countries. Even more important, I chose Hansberry because, through *A Raisin in the Sun*, she changed the face of African American theater. The historical production was accompanied by several other firsts. Lloyd Richards became the first black director on Broadway of a play by and about blacks with essentially a black cast (Abramson 241). The show was financially successful. And, for the first time, African American people went to the theater in great numbers. Opening on Broadway on March 11, 1959, *A Raisin in the Sun* successfully ran for 538 performances and has since become a classic (Hornby 31).

Critics credit a variety of reasons for the success of *A Raisin in the Sun* ranging from the first positive portrayal of an African male figure to Hansberry's thorough treatment of a variety of socio-political issues. Hansberry once wrote: "All art is ultimately socio-political. . . . The writer is deceived who thinks he has some other choice. The question is not whether one will make a social statement in one's work— but only what the statement will say, for if it says anything, it will be social" (5). In works like *A Raisin in the Sun* and *Les Blancs*, Hansberry said it was not feasible for African Americans to turn their heads to racism; she said it was not reasonable to allow greed to disrupt family life; and she said it was not suitable for African American writers to perpetuate false stereotypes of African Americans or Africans. Through Hansberry's portrayal of the African character Asagi in *A Raisin in the Sun*, "With the pen," Brown-Guillory notes, "Hansberry destroyed the myth [about the African male], perpetuated by the media, of the wild, savage, ugly, naked creature given to carnivorous pillaging. For this alone Hansberry deserves a permanent place in American theater history" (36).

A masterfully woven drama, *A Raisin in the Sun* aggressively tackles a plethora of issues, all without any of them seeming forced. Through the framing techniques she employs, by the drama's end, Hansberry has called attention to the differences created by generation gaps, to the conflicts that arise because of competing ideologies, to males' sexist treatment of women, to the concept of African Americans' assimilation into a European-based culture, to the colonialism in Africa which in many ways, still exists in countries in Africa, to abortion, to integration, to the deferred American dream, and to greed. But because Walter's failure and suffering are so much the focal point of the drama, most of these issues become peripheral, as is characteristic of dramatic frames. Each frame supports the central figure while possessing a center of its own. In no other place in American theatre have so many important issues been so well integrated into one drama. While the Youngers may have far more problems than any one family would like to have, in many ways, they are *every* family trying to deal with everyday situations. They are hard-working, law-abiding dreamers who know first hand what happens to a dream deferred. Their job is to remind us, as Mama tells Beneatha, that "when you starts measuring somebody, measure him right, child, measure him right. Make sure you done taken into account what hills and valleys he come through before he got to wherever he is" (Hansberry 125). Taking into account the "hills and valleys," Hansberry , as a young, gifted, and black *female*, has come through, the skill with which she composed her dramas, especially *A Raisin in the Sun*, is nothing short of brilliant.

Although Alice Childress precedes Hansberry as a published playwright, I have included Childress because her work continues for years after the death of Hansberry. In fact, Childress is the only African American female playwright in America whose plays have been written, produced, and published over a period of five decades. Even more notable is that Childress accomplished this without compromising her beliefs. Much like the character Wileta from her first full-length drama, *Trouble in Mind* (1955), Childress refused to conform to the powers-that-be at the expense of personal integrity. During the early years of her writing career, Childress composed her "Mildred" sketches, which were eventually published in *Like One of the Family . . . Conversations for a Domestic's Life*. These sketches, arguably inspired by Langston Hughes' "Simple," were originally written for Paul Robeson's *Freedom*. At least somewhat aware of Robeson's problems with the United States government and of his link to the Communist Party, Childress opted to continue a relationship with Robeson and with *Freedom*, which many critics argue contributed tremendously to her critical obscurity. But as time progressed, Childress became more accepted in theatre and scholarly circles, though she has yet to receive the amount of scholarly criticism deserving of such a fine-tuned and socially conscious playwright.

Childress's second full-length serious drama, *Wedding Band: A Love/Hate Story in Black and White* (1973), is, perhaps, one of the most under-acknowledged plays in all of feminist drama. Exploring what Childress has called the "anti-woman" laws which governed the South after Reconstruction, *Wedding Band* dramatizes the relationship between a black woman named Julia and her white lover Herman. Set in 1918 in Childress's birthplace, Charleston, South Carolina, the drama shows how inhumane anti-woman laws which prohibited legal miscegenation and divorce and which dispossessed black women from their property rights complement inhumanity to make life virtually unbearable for black and white women alike. Childress, as quoted in Rosemary Curb, remarks:

> The play [*Wedding Band*] shows society's determination to hold the black woman down through laws framed against her. There are similar laws framed against white women, and, of course, unwritten laws. I never run out of subject matter for writing about women's rights—particularly black women, but white women too, which I have included in *Wedding Band*. (59)

Completely ignoring the underlying theme which Childress tries to convey with *Wedding Band*, an overwhelming amount of the criticism on the drama ignores its feminist undertakings and focuses on the fact that it depicts an interracial relationship in the segregated South. But according to Childress, what is most important about the drama is that it exposes the denial of women's rights by laws created by men to protect men. Because of the "anti-woman" laws, Julia is unable to marry Herman; Mattie is denied family benefits from the Merchant Marines because the state of South Carolina prohibits divorce and, thus, denies the legality of her second marriage to the marine; and Herman's mother must jeopardize his life by waiting until it is dark to transport the influenza-stricken Herman from Julia's house to the doctor for fear of laws that would question a white man's presence in a black neighborhood and outside of a required quarantine. Thus, both her black and white female characters become victims of a patriarchal system which shuns them because of race, because of class, and because of gender.

Though its subject matter was thought to be too common to warrant a Broadway appearance, *Wedding Band* reached an ever larger audience than Broadway when it was televised nationally on ABC in 1974. However, it has yet to be fully recognized for its significance as feminist protest literature, unveiling the unnecessary difficulties women encounter because of laws men impose on them.

While Hansberry and Childress's portrayal of women as independent and strong-willed helped set the stage for future playwrights like Adrienne Kennedy and Ntozake Shange, these dramatists handle similar subject matter quite differently from their playwrighting predecessors. Perhaps most accurately labeled as postmodernists, Kennedy and Shange's female characters shared a quest for identity. But as much as Kennedy and Shange differ from Hansberry and Childress, they differ from one another. Subscribing to the more traditional postmodern conventions, Kennedy's protagonists seldom establish the holistic identities they seek, while Shange's female characters eventually achieve the wholeness they desire.

The one undertaking that is, perhaps, most descriptive of all postmodernist thought and its subsequent literature is its tendency to subvert the foundations of traditional thought. While the means by which postmodernists achieve this subversion varies among authors, their primary aims is to show the instability of stability, the uncertainty of certainty, the meaninglessness of meaning. Thus, the reader of post-modern literature constantly finds herself trying to figure out "Which world is this?" It is this very question that the audience of an Adrienne Kennedy finds itself asking. Particularly in *Funnyhouse of the Negro* (1962), the audience queries "Which world is this? Which one of her *selves* are we encountering now?" In this sense, Kennedy's drama can be labeled postmodern as accurately as it has been labeled surrealist, self-reflexive, or mimetic.

Rejecting the traditional conception of self, Sarah, the Negro of the drama's title, discursively struggles to find her own identity, ultimately rejecting all possibilities. Rather than deal with reality, Kennedy's protagonist creates her own existence. Negro-Sarah has four selves, as the Duchess of Hapsburg, as Queen Victoria Regina, as Jesus, and as Patrice Lumumba. She can no longer believe in the hopes and dreams of the ordinary woman because, for each of her selves, they have proven to be lies. Susan Meigs suggests, that through characters like Sarah, "Kennedy exposes how black Americans, especially women, having been denied a social context and history, are therefore powerless to resolve the chaotic elements of their black female identities" (173). Such is the case with Sarah. She confesses, "I try to create a space for myselves in cities . . . but it becomes a lie. I try to give myselves a logical relationship but that too is a lie . . . A loving relationship exists between myself and Queen Victoria, a love between myself and Jesus but they are lies" (Kennedy 7). Unable to decipher lies from the truth, the real from the unreal, Sarah is unable to resolve her self-hatred and the subsequent fragmentation of her self.

Like Kennedy, Shange can be accurately labeled as a postmodern dramatist. Attempting to escape the stifling bounds of tradition, Shange writes in the preface of *Three Pieces*, "I cant count the number of times I have viscerally wanted to attack deform n maim the language that I waz taught to hate myself in" (xii). This desire to establish a nonwhite non-European language form manifests itself in her best-known dramatic choreopoem *for colored girls who have considered suicide/ when the rainbow is enuf* (1977) through the poet's use of non-traditional syntax and orthography and her use of verbal "distortions." Like Kennedy's protagonists,

Shange's female characters in *for colored girls* are in search of an identity independent of their designated role as "other." But unlike Sarah-Negro, each of the seven women in *for colored girls* is able to resolve her psychic crisis and emancipate herself. Shange argues that this liberation would be impossible outside of a collective voice; thus, while the drama does portray the lives of seven very different women, it is ultimately concerned with the collective experience and the communal expression that allows these women to defeat the stress of racism and to overcome feelings of rage, defeat, and frustration.

In sum, although the patriarchal mind set of those who determine the American drama canon is a contributing factor to the frequent exclusion of African American female playwrights in production and publication, it is not the lone determinant. Black theater companies are heavily dependent on outside funding, specifically agencies such as the various state arts councils and the federally-sponsored National Endowment for the Arts (NEA) (Bailey 319-322). Consequently, when government funding becomes limited, frequency of and accessibility to any African American theater becomes limited as well. Thus, the African American theater must vastly decrease its interdependence on foundation and government funding to ensure its presence and survival. With stronger support from theater goers, African American drama must begin to gain the independence essential for it to thrive and to flourish. Equally as important as support from theatre-goers is support from university students, professors, and scholars. At African American universities, where drama departments are performing well-produced dramas, more often than not, a majority of the seats are left unoccupied or are filled only one night of many performances. Very seldom are dramas included in university African American literature syllabi, as drama is seemingly considered "substandard" literature. Undeniably, it is held in far less esteem than the great African American novel or even the highly expressive African American book of poetry. To allow African American theatre to grow and to flourish and to achieve its invaluable place in the African American literary canon, scholars must give dramatists critical attention and university professors must include them in their course syllabi, and this inclusion cannot be limited to August Wilson and other male dramatists. The many female playwrights included in this bibliography must also hold a place in African literature. The role of the artist in ensuring both the production and the publication of her work, as well as her inclusion in university syllabi, is to provide, consistently, theater-goers and readers with quality material. As drama critic A. Peter Bailey asserts, artists "must do more than 'tell it like it is.' Instead, they must strive to tell the whole truth about the people of whom they write, dealing with their strengths as well as their weaknesses, their heroes as well as their outlaws; with Wall Street and international affairs as well as Harlem and South-Side Chicago; with love relationships as well as warped ones" (322).

The playwrights included in this bibliography do much more than "tell it like it is." They have attempted to tell "why it is like it is," and better yet, what happens "when it is like it is." To them, all the world's a stage; to make them headliners is my only hope.

WORKS CITED

Abramson, Doris. *Negro Playwrights in the American Theater, 1925-1959*. New York: Columbia University Press, 1969.

Bailey, A. Peter. "A Look at the Contemporary Black Theatre Movement." *Dictionary of Literary Biography: Afro-American Writers after 1955 (Dramatists and Prose Writers)*. Vol. 38. Detroit: Gale, 1925. 319-322. Rpt. From *Black American Literature Forum* 17 (Spring 1983): 19-21.

Brown-Guillory, Elizabeth. *Their Place on the Stage: Black Women Playwrights in America*. New York: Praeger, 1988.

Curb, Rosemary. "An Unfashionable Tragedy of American Racism: Alice Childress's *Wedding Band*." *Melus* 7 (Winter 1980): 57-68.

Hansberry, Lorraine. *A Raisin in the Sun*. New York: Signet, 1966.

————. "The Negro Writer and His Roots: Toward a New Romanticism." *The Black Scholar* 12 (March/April 1981): 5.

Hornby, Richard. *Drama, Metadrama, and Perception*. Lewisburg, PA: Bucknell University Press, 1986.

Kennedy, Adrienne. *Funnyhouse of the Negro. Adrienne Kennedy in One Act*. Minneapolis, MN: U of Minnesota P, 1988. 1-23.

Mahone, Sydné. *Moon Marked and Touched by Sun: Plays by African-American Women*. New York: Theatre Communications Group, 1994.

Meigs, Susan. "No Place but the Funnyhouse: The Struggle for Identity in Three Adrienne Kennedy Plays." *Modern American Drama: The Female Canon*. Ed. June Schleuter. Rutherford, NJ: Fairleigh Dickinson U P, 1990. 172-183.

Shange, Ntozake. Foreword. *three pieces*. New York: St. Martin's Press, 1981.

I ANTHOLOGIES

The following is a list of selected anthologies that include one or more plays by contemporary African American female playwrights.

A1.   Adams, William, Peter Conn, and Barry Slepian, eds. *Afro-American Literature: Drama*. Boston: Houghton Mifflin, 1970.

Contains Lorraine Hansberry's *A Raisin in the Sun*.

A2.   Altenbernd, Lynn, ed. *Exploring Literature: Fiction, Drama, Criticism*. New York: Macmillan, 1970.

Contains five dramas, one of which is Lorraine Hansberry's *A Raisin in the Sun*.

A3.   Anderson, T. Dianne. *The Unicorn Died at Dawn*. Lutz, FL: Anderson Publishing, 1981.

Contains the following dramas by Anderson: *Come Yesterday, Just Friendly, Nightcap, Home to Roost, Closing Time, The Unicorn Died at Dawn, Black Sparrow, Cyro,* and *The Gift of Hurmonia*.

A4.   Baraka, Amiri, and Amina Baraka, eds. *Confirmation: An Anthology of African American Women*. New York: William Morrow, 1983.

Includes poetry, short stories, and dramas of African American women. Aishah Rahman's *Lady and the Tramp* and *Transcendental Blues* are the only two dramas anthologized.

A5.   Barranger, M.S., and Daniel Dodson, eds. *Generations: An Introduction to Drama*. New York: Harcourt Brace Jovanovich, 1971.

        Contains Lorraine Hansberry's *A Raisin in the Sun*.

A6.   Barnes, Clive, ed. *Best American Plays: Eighth Series 1974-1982*. New York: Crown, 1983.

        Contains seventeen dramas, one of which is Ntozake Shange's *for colored girls who have considered suicide/when the rainbow is enuf*.

A7.   Booker, Merrel D., Sr., et al., eds. *Cry at Birth*. New York: McGraw-Hill, 1971.

        Contains *The Flags* by Sue Booker.

A8.   Branch, William B., ed. *Black Thunder: An Anthology of Contemporary African-American Drama*. New York: Penguin Group, 1992.

        Contains nine dramas by African American playwrights, one of which is P.J. Gibson's *Long Time Since Yesterday*.

A9.   Brasmer, William, and Dominick Consolo, eds. *Black Drama: An Anthology*. Columbus: Merrill Publishing, 1970.

        Contains six dramas, one of which is Adrienne Kennedy's *Funnyhouse of a Negro*.

A10.   Brown-Guillory, Elizabeth, ed. *Wines in the Wilderness: Plays by African American Women from the Harlem Renaissance to the Present*. Westport, CT: Greenwood Press, 1990.

        Contains thirteen dramas by African American women. Those published after 1959 are Sonia Sanchez's *Sister Son/ji*, Sybil Kein's *Get Together*, and Elizabeth Brown-Guillory's *Mam Phyllis*.

A11.   Bullins, Ed, ed. *New Plays from the Black Theatre: An Anthology*. New York: Bantam Books, 1969.

        Contains eleven dramas by African American playwrights, one of which is Sonia Sanchez's *Sister Son/ji*.

A12.   ———, ed. *The New Lafayette Theatre Presents Plays With Aesthetic Comments by Six Black Playwrights*. Garden City: Anchor Press, 1974.

Contains six dramas, one of which is Sonia Sanchez's *Uh, Uh: But How Do It Free Us?*

A13.   Cassady, Marshall, and Pat Cassady, eds. *An Introduction to Theatre and Drama*. Skokie, IL: National Textbook, 1975.

Contains thirteen dramas, one of which is Lorraine Hansberry's *A Raisin in the Sun*.

A14.   Cerf, Bennett, ed. *Four Contemporary American Plays*. New York: Vintage/ Random House, 1961.

Contains four dramas, one of which is Lorraine Hansberry's *A Raisin in the Sun*.

A15.   ———, ed. *Six American Plays for Today*. New York: Random House, 1961.

Lorraine Hansberry's *A Raisin in the Sun*.

A16.   ———, ed. *Plays for Our Time*. New York: Random House, 1967.

Contains Lorraine Hansberry's *A Raisin in the Sun*.

A17.   Childress, Alice, ed. *Black Scenes*. Garden City, NY: Zenith Books, 1971.

Contains a collection of scenes from fifteen African American dramas, three of which are Hansberry's *A Raisin in the Sun*, Childress's *The African Garden*, and Abbey Lincoln's *A Streak o' Lean*.

A18.   ———, ed. *Mojo and String: Two Plays*. New York: Dramatists Play Service, 1971.

Includes two of Childress's dramas, *Mojo* and *String*.

A19.   Clark, China (Debra). *Neffie and In Sorrow's Room* (Unverified title). New York: Era Publishing Co., 1976.

Includes two of Clark's dramas, *Neffie* and *In Sorrow's Room*.

A20.   Couch, William, ed. *New Playwrights, An Anthology*. Baton Rouge: Louisiana State University Press, 1968.

Contains six dramas, one of which is Adrienne Kennedy's *A Rat's Mass*.

A21.   Davis, Arthur P., and J. Saunders Redding, eds. *Cavalcade: Negro American Writing from 1760 to the Present*. Boston: Houghton Mifflin, 1971.

Contains a collection of writings of African Americans from 1760 to the present, one of which is Sonia Sanchez's *The Bronx Is Next*.

A22.   Dietrich, Richard F., William Carpenter, and Kevin Kerrance, eds. *The Art of Drama*. New York: Holt, Rinehart and Winston, 1969.

Contains Lorraine Hansberry's *A Raisin in the Sun*.

A23.   ———, eds. *The Realities of Literature*. Waltham, MA: Xerox College Press, 1971.

Contains Lorraine Hansberry's *A Raisin in the Sun*.

A24.   *The Drama Review* (Black Theatre Issue) 12 (Summer 1968).

Contains Dorothy Ahmad's *Papa's Daughter* and Sonia Sanchez's *The Bronx Is Next*.

A25.   Gassner, John, and Clive Barnes, eds. *The Best American Plays, 6th Series: 1963-1967*. New York: Crown, 1971.

Contains seventeen dramas, one of which is Lorraine Hansberry's *The Sign in Sidney Brustein's Window*.

A26.   Griffith, Francis, and Joseph Mersand, eds. *Eight American Ethnic Plays*. New York: Scribner's, 1974.

Contains Lorraine Hansberry's *A Raisin in the Sun*.

A27.   Hansberry, Lorraine. *A Raisin in the Sun and The Sign in Sidney Brustein's Window*. New York: New American Library, 1987.

Contains Hansberry's dramas *A Raisin in the Sun* and *The Sign in Sidney Brustein's Window*.

A28.   ———. *Les Blancs: The Collected Last Plays of Lorraine Hansberry*. New York: Random House, 1972; Vintage, 1973.

Contains Hansberry's *Les Blancs*, *The Drinking Gourd*, and *What Use Are the Flowers?*

A29.   Harrison, Paul Carter, ed. *Kuntu Drama: Plays of the African Continuum*. New York: Grove Press, 1974.

Contains nine dramas, two of which are Adrienne Kennedy's *The Owl Answers* and *A Beast's Story*.

A30.   ———, ed. *Totem Voices: Plays from the Black World Repertory*. New York: Grove Press, 1989.

Contains nine dramas by black playwrights, one of which is Ntozake Shange's *for colored girls who considered suicide/when the rainbow is enuf.*

A31.   Hatch, James V., ed. *Black Theater USA: Forty-Five Plays by Black Americans, 1847-1974*. New York: The Free Press, 1974.

Contains forty-five dramas by African American playwrights. Section 11, "Modern Black Women," includes Lorraine Hansberry's *The Drinking Gourd*, Alice Childress's *Wines in the Wilderness*, Adrienne Kennedy's *The Owl Answers* and Martie Charles's *Job Security.*

A32.   Heisch, Elizabeth, ed. *Discovery and Recollection: An Anthology of Literary Types*. New York: Holt, Rinehart, and Winston, 1970.

Contains Lorraine Hansberry's *A Raisin in the Sun* among over one hundred entries of poems, short stories, and dramas.

A33.   Hoffman, William, ed. *New American Plays*. Vol. 2. New York: Nill & Wang, 1968.

Contains Adrienne Kennedy's *The Owl Answers.*

A34.   Jones, LeRoi, and Larry Neal, eds. *Black Fire: An Anthology of Afro-American Writings*. New York: William Morrow, 1968.

Contains a collection of essays, poetry, fiction, and drama. Ten dramas are anthologized, one of which is *The Suicide* by Carol Freeman.

A35.   Jones, Lola E. *Three Plays*. New York: Exposition Press, 1965. Rpt. as *Fatal Female Figures in Three Plays*. Baltimore: Morgan State Univ., 1983.

Contains Jones's dramas entitled *The Other Side of the Wall, The Places of Wrath*, and *Helen*.

A36.   ———. *Exploring the Black Experience in America*. Franklin Square, NY: F. Peters 1976. Rpt. Baltimore: Morgan State University Press, 1976.

Contains Jones's dramas entitled *The New Nigger, or Who's Afraid of William Faulkner?* and *The Deal*.

A37.   Kennedy, Adrienne. *Cities in Bezique: Two One-Act Plays*. New York: Samuel French, 1969.

Contains Kennedy's *The Owl Answers* and *A Beast's Story*.

A38.   ———. *Adrienne Kennedy in One Act*. Minneapolis: University of Minnesota Press, 1988.

Contains the following dramas by Kennedy: *Funnyhouse of a Negro, The Owl Answers, A Lesson in Dead Language, A Rat's Mass, Sun, A Movie Star Has to Star in Black and White*, and the Greek adaptations *Electra* and *Orestes*.

A39.   ———. *The Alexander Plays*. Minneapolis: University of Minnesota Press, 1992.

Contains the following dramas by Kennedy: *She Talks to Beethoven, The Ohio State Murders, The Film Club (A Monologue by Suzanne Alexander)*, and *The Dramatic Circle*, each of which details some experience in the life of Kennedy's recurring dramatic character Suzanne Alexander.

A40.   King, Woodie, Jr., ed. *New Plays for the Black Theatre*. Chicago: Third World Press, 1989.

Contains fifteen dramas, four of which are Elois Beasley's *The Fallen Angel*, Pearl Cleage's *Hospice*, P. J. Gibson's *Konvergence*, Nubia Kai's *Parting*, and Ntozake Shange's *Daddy Says*.

A41.   King, Woodie, Jr., and Ron Milner, eds. *Black Drama Anthology*. New York: Penguin Group, 1971

Anthologizes twenty-three dramas, two of which are Martie Charles's *Black Cycle* and Elaine Jackson's *Toe Jam*.

A42.   Mahone, Sydné, ed. *Moon Marked and Touched by Sun: Plays by Afri-can-American Women*. New York: Theatre Communications Group, 1994.

Contains Laurie Carlos's *White Chocolate for My Father*, Kia Corthron's *Cage Rhythm*, Thulani Davis's *X*, Judith Alexa Jackson's *WOMBman-WARs*, Adrienne Kennedy's *The Dramatic Circle*, Robbie McCauley's *Sally's Rape*, Suzan-Lori Parks's *The Death of the Last Black Man in the Whole Entire World*, Aishah Rahman's *The Mojo and the Sayso*, excerpts from Ntozake Shange's *The Resurrection of the Daughter: Liliane*, excerpts from Anna Deavere Smith's *Fires in the Mirror*, and Danitra Vance's *Live and In Color!*

A43.   Marranca, Bonnie, and Gautam Dasgupta, eds. *Word Plays 3: New American Drama*. New York: Performing Arts Journal Publications, 1984.

Contains six dramas, one of which is Adrienne Kennedy's *A Movie Star Has to Star in Black and White*.

A44.   Miles, Julia, ed. *The Women's Project: The American Place Theatre*. New York: Performing Arts Journal Publications & American Place Theatre, 1980.

Contains Kathleen Collins's *In the Midnight Hour*.

A45.   ———, ed. *Playwriting Women: Seven Plays from the Women's Project*. Portsmouth, NY: Heinemann, 1993.

Contains seven dramas, two of which are Pearl Cleage's *Chain* and *Late Bus to Mecca*.

A46.   Moore, Honor, ed. *The New Women's Theatre: Ten Plays by Contempo-rary American Women*. New York: Vintage Books, 1977.

Contains ten dramas, one of which is Alice Childress's *The Wedding Band*.

A47.   Oliver, Clinton F., and Stephanie Sills, eds. *Contemporary Black Drama: From* A Raisin in the Sun *to* No Place To Be Somebody. New York: Charles Scribner's Sons, 1971.

Includes eight dramas, two of which are Hansberry's *A Raisin in the Sun* and Adrienne Kennedy's *Funnyhouse of a Negro*.

A48.   O'Neal, Regina. *And Then the Harvest: Three Television Plays*. Detroit: Broadside Press, 1974.

Contains O'Neal's *Walk a Tight Rope, And Then the Harvest,* and *Night Watch*.

A49.   Ostrow, Eileen J., ed. *Center Stage: An Anthology of Twenty-One Contemporary Black-American Plays*. Oakland: Sea Urchin Press, 1981.

Anthologizes *Loners* by J. California Cooper, *The Fisherman* by Dianne Houston, *Revival* by Lee Hunkins, *In the Master's House There Are Many Mansions* by Cherry Jackson, *The Moving Violation* by Sharon Stockard Martin, *The Trip* by Crystal Rhodes, *No One Man Show* by Thelma Jackson Stiles, *Hands in the Mirror* by Leona N. Welch, and *A Christmas Story* by Anita Jane Williams.

A50.   Parone, Edward. *Collision Course: An Omnibus of Seventeen Brief Plays*. New York: Random House, 1968.

Contains seventeen dramas, one of which is Adrienne Kennedy's *A Lesson in Dead Language*.

A51.   Patterson, Lindsay, ed. *Anthology of the American Negro in the Theatre*. New York: Publisher's Co, 1967.

Contains Adrienne Kennedy's *Funnyhouse of a Negro*. Also contains critical or scholarly information on Negro theatre. Consult the index to find brief comments on contemporary African American female playwrights.

A52.   ———, ed. *Black Theater: A Twentieth Century Collection of the Work of Its Best Playwrights*. New York: Dodd, Mead, and Co., 1971.

Contains twelve dramas, one of which is Hansberry's *A Raisin in the Sun*.

A53.   Richards, Stanley, ed. *The Best Short Plays of the World Theatre, 1968-1973*. New York: Crown, 1973.

Contains twenty dramas, one of which is Alice Childress's *Mojo*.

A54.   Sanchez, Sonia, ed. *Three Hundred and Sixty Degrees of Blackness Comin' at You*. New York: 5X Publishing, 1971.

Contains *The Light* by Dolores Abramson, *Hoodoo Talkin* by Susan Batson, and *Moma Don't Know What Love Is* by Nia nSabe.

A55.   Shange, Ntozake. *Three Pieces*. New York: St. Martin's Press, 1981;
        Rpt. New York: Penguin Books, 1982.

        Contains Shange's *spell #7*, *A Photograph: Lovers-in-Motion*, and
        Boogie Woogie Landscapes.

A56.   ———. *Plays, One*. London: Methuen Drama, 1992.

        Contains Shange's *for colored girls*, *spell #7*, *The Love Space Demands*,
        and *I Heard Eric Dolphy in His Eyes*.

A57.   Simonson, Harold, ed. *Quartet: A Book of Stories, Plays, Poems, and
        Critical Essays*. New York: Harper and Row, 1973.

        Contains over two-hundred entries of stories, plays, poems, and critical
        essays. Of the six plays anthologized, Lorraine Hansberry's *A Raisin in
        the Sun* is the only drama by a contemporary African American female
        playwright.

A58.   ———, ed. *Ensemble Studio Theatre (EST) Marathon 1994: One Act
        Plays*. Lyme, NH: Smith & Kraus, 1995.

        Contains twelve dramas, one of which is Regina Taylor's *Mudtracks*.

A59.   Smith, Michael, ed. *More Plays from Off-Off-Broadway*. Indianapolis:
        Bobbs-Merrill, 1966.

        Contains Adrienne Kennedy's *A Rat's Mass*.

A60.   Sullivan, Victoria, and James V. Hatch, eds. *Plays by and about Wo-
        men*. New York: Random House, 1973.

        Contains eight dramas, one of which is *Wine in the Wilderness* by Alice
        Childress.

A61.   Symes, Ken M., ed. *Two Voices: Writing about Literature*. Boston:
        Houghton Mifflin, 1976.

        Contains Lorraine Hansberry's *A Raisin in the Sun*.

A62.   Turner, Darwin, ed. *Black Drama in America: An Anthology*. Washing-
        ton: Howard University, 1994.

        Contains fourteen dramas, two of which are J.E. Franklin's *Miss Honey's
        Young'uns* and Pearl Cleage's *Flyin' West*.

A63.   Walker, Lucy M. *Social Action in One-Act Plays*. Denver: Privately printed, 1970.

Contains the following dramas by Walker: *It's Only Money, A Dollar a Day Keeps the Doctor Away, We All Play, My Own Man, The Real Estate Man, To Cuss or Bus*, and *Grades—Plus or Minus*.

A64.   White, Melvin, and Frank Whiting, eds. *Playreader's Repertory: An Anthology for Introduction to the Theatre*. Glenview, IL: Scott, Foresman, 1970.

Contains fourteen dramas, one of which is Lorraine Hansberry's *A Raisin in the Sun*.

A65.   Wilkerson, Margaret B., ed. *Nine Plays by Black Women*. New York: Penguin Books, 1986.

Contains *A Black Woman Speaks* by Beah Richards, *Toussaint: Excerpt from Act I of a Work in Progress* by Lorraine Hansberry, *The Wedding Band* by Alice Childress, *The Tapestry* by Alexis DeVeaux, *Unfinished Women Cry in No Man's Land While a Bird Dies in a Gilded Cage* by Aishah Rahman, *spell #7: geechee jibara quick magic trance manual for technologically stressed third world people: A Theater Piece* by Ntozake Shange, *The Brothers* by Kathleen Collins, *Paper Dolls* by Elaine Jackson, and *Brown Silk and Magenta Sunsets* by P.J. Gibson.

II GENERAL CRITICISM AND REFERENCE WORKS

The following are general critical works and reference works that make substantive reference to contemporary African American female playwrights and their plays.

B1.   Abramson, Doris E. *Negro Playwrights in the American Theatre, 1925-1959*. New York: Columbia Univ. Press, 1969.

Highlights the personal experiences and dramas of African American playwrights from 1925-1959. Significant attention is given to Lorraine Hansberry, including the direct experiences of her life that are portrayed in her dramas. Consult the thorough index for other references to Hansberry and Adrienne Kennedy.

B2.   Arata, Esther S. *More Black American Playwrights: A Bibliography*. Metuchen, NJ: Scarecrow Press, 1978.

Lists published plays of African American dramatists with criticism and reviews on plays through 1978. It is a continuation of Arata and Rotoli's 1976 bibliography.

B3.   Arata, Esther S., and Nicholas Rotoli. *Black American Playwrights, 1800 to the Present: A Bibliography*. Metuchen, NJ: Scarecrow Press, 1976.

Lists published plays of African American dramatists with criticism and reviews on plays through 1975.

B4.   Betsko, Kathleen, and Rachel Koenig. *Interviews with Contemporary Women Playwrights*. New York: Beach Tree Books, 1987.

Includes interviews with thirty contemporary British, American, Chinese, Argentine, and French women dramatists. The three contemporary African American female playwrights included are Alice Childress, Adrienne Kennedy, and Ntozake Shange.

B5.   Bigelow, Barbara C., ed. *Contemporary Black Biography: Profiles from the International Black Community.* 6 vols. Detroit: Gale Research, 1994.

Contains profiles on Rita Dove, Lorraine Hansberry, Abbey Lincoln, and Anna Deavere Smith.

B6.   Blackshire-Belay, Carol A., ed. *Language and Literature in the African American Imagination.* Westport, CT: Greenwood, 1992.

Contains fourteen essays on African American language and literature, two of which are Barbara Marshall's "Kitchen Table Talk: J. California Cooper's Use of Nommo-Female Binding Transcendence" and Geta LeSeur's "From Nice Colored Girl to Womanist: An Exploration of Development in Ntozake Shange's Writings."

B7.   Bloom, Harold, ed. *Black American Women Poets and Dramatists.* New York: Chelsea House, 1996.

According to the user's guide, this volume "provides biographical, critical, and bibliographical information on the seventeen most significant black American women poets and dramatists. Each chapter consists of three parts: a biography of the author; a selection of brief critical extracts about the author; and a bibliography of the author's published books" (vi). Contemporary African American dramatists included are Alice Childress, Rita Dove, Lorraine Hansberry, Sonia Sanchez, and Ntozake Shange.

B8.   Bock, Hedwig, and Albert Wertheim, eds. *Essays on Contemporary American Drama.* Munich: M. Hueber, 1981.

Introduces readers to the contemporary American theatre. Includes Margaret Wilkerson's "The Sighted Eyes and Feeling Heart of Lorraine Hansberry" and Patti P. Gillespie's essay "American Women Dramatists, 1960-1980" which examines the work of women playwrights writing and producing plays during the late 50s through the 70s including Adrienne Kennedy and Ntozake Shange.

B9.   Bowles, Juliette, ed. *In Memory and Spirit of Frances, Zora, and Lorraine: Essays and Interviews on Black Women and Writing.* Washington, DC: Institute for the Arts and the Humanities, Howard Univ., 1979.

Contains interviews with four African American writers, one of whom is Ntozake Shange with James Early; proceedings from the 1978 (Institute for Arts and Humanities) Writers Conference Panel, "Black Women Writers and Feminism"; essays from Friends of the Institute for Arts and Humanities (FIAH); and a section on Representations of Black Women in Literature and Mass Media.

B10.   Brater, Enoch, ed. *Feminine Focus: The New Women Playwrights.* Cambridge: Oxford Univ. Press, 1989.

Contains fifteen essays, two of which are "Distraught Laughter: Monologue in Ntozake Shange's Theater Pieces" by Deborah Geis and "Rites and Responsibilities: The Drama of Black American Women" by Helene Keyssar.

B11.   Brown, Janet. *Feminist Drama: Definition and Critical Analysis.* Metuchen, NJ: Scarecrow Press, 1979.

Includes eight chapters of critical analysis on feminist drama, two of which are *"Wine in the Wilderness"* and *"for colored girls who considered suicide."*

B12.   Brown-Guillory, Elizabeth. *Their Place on the Stage: Black Women Playwrights in America.* New York: Praeger, 1988.

Examines the dramatic tradition of African American women from the Harlem Renaissance to the present. Brown-Guillory pays special attention to Alice Childress, Lorraine Hansberry, and Ntozake Shange.

B13.   Carroll, Rebecca, ed. *I Know What the Red Clay Looks Like: The Voice and Vision of Black Women Writers.* New York: Crown Publishers, 1994.

Contains essays written by black women writers on the experiences that influenced their writing and on contemporary issues. The collection also includes brief excerpts from their selected works. Contemporary dramatists featured are Pearl Cleage and J. California Cooper.

B14.   Case, Sue-Ellen. *Feminism and Theatre.* New York: Methuen, 1988.

Provides a helpful introduction to feminist theatre. Case's concentration is on playwrights she considers feminist or works that she considers feminist texts. Consult the index for brief mention of contemporary African American female playwrights like Alice Childress, Lorraine Hansberry, Adrienne Kennedy, Sonia Sanchez, and Ntozake Shange.

B15.   Chinoy, Helen K., and Linda Walsh Jenkins, eds. *Women in American Theatre*. New York: Theatre Communications Group, 1987.

Examines the role of women in theatre in over fifty essays by noted drama critics and feminists. Includes the following essays on contemporary African American female playwrights: "'Lesson I Bleed': Adrienne Kennedy's Blood Rites" by Rosemary K. Curb; "Black Women in Plays by Black Playwrights" by Jeanne-Marie A. Miller; "Who Put the Tragic in the Tragic Mulatto?" by Winona L. Fletcher; and "A Rainbow of Voices" by Phyllis Mael.

B16.   Christ, Carol P. *Diving Deep and Surfacing: Women Writers on Spiritual Quest*. Boston: Beacon Press, 1980.

Contains eight chapters on women writers, one of which is "'i found god in myself . . . & loved her fiercely': Ntozake Shange."

B17.   Cohn, Ruby. *New American Dramatists: 1960-1980*. New York: Grove Press, 1982.

Contains ten chapters of essays, one of which is "Black on Black: Baraka, Bullins, Kennedy." The essay includes brief examinations of the following Kennedy plays: *Funnyhouse of a Negro, The Owl Answers, A Rat's Mass, A Lesson in Dead Language, An Evening with Dead Essex,* and *A Movie Star Has to Be Born in Black and White.*

B18.   Coven, Brenda. *American Women Dramatists of the Twentieth Century: A Bibliography*. Metuchen, NJ: Scarecrow, 1982.

Lists plays (published and unpublished), biographies, and drama reviews of the following contemporary African American female playwrights: Vinnette Carroll, Alice Childress, Micki Grant, Lorraine Hansberry, Adrienne Kennedy, and Ntozake Shange.

B19.   Davis, Thadious, and Trudier Harris, eds. *Dictionary of Literary Biography: Afro-American Writers after 1955, Dramatists and Prose Writers*. Vol. 38. Detroit: Gale Research Co., 1985.

Includes biographical sketches and playwright profiles for the following contemporary African American female playwrights: Alice Childress, Alexis DeVeaux, Lorraine Hansberry, Adrienne Kennedy, and Ntozake Shange.

B20.   Evans, Mari, ed. *Black Women Writers (1950-1980): A Critical Evaluation*. Garden City, NY: Anchor Books, 1984.

Includes essays by and about Alice Childress, Gayl Jones, and Sonia Sanchez. Those related to drama are: "Alice Childress's Dramatic Structure," by Samuel Hay; "The Literary Genius of Alice Childress," by John O. Killens; "About My Work," by Gayl Jones; and "Sonia Sanchez: The Bringer of Memories," by Haki Madhubuti.

B21.   Fabre, Genevieve. *Afro-American Poetry and Drama, 1760-1975: A Guide to Information Sources*. Detroit: Gale Research Co., 1979.

Provides a listing of relevant library sources, periodicals, bibliographies, play collections, critical studies, as well as bibliographic information on published and unpublished plays and biographical sources and criticism on or by African American dramatists. Contemporary female playwrights featured are Alice Childress, Lorraine Hansberry, Adrienne Kennedy, and Sonia Sanchez.

B22.   ————. *Drumbeats, Masks and Metaphors: Contemporary Afro-American Theatre*. Cambridge: Harvard University Press, 1983.

Makes substantive references to the following contemporary African American female playwrights: Vinnette Carroll, Alice Childress, Lorraine Hansberry, Adrienne Kennedy, Sonia Sanchez, and Ntozake Shange. Consult the index for individual playwrights found in one of the four chapters entitled "The Historical Precedent," "The Militant Theatre," "Theatre of Experience," and "Theatre of Culture."

B23.   Gates, Henry Louis, Jr., ed. *Reading Black, Reading Feminist*. New York: Meridian, 1990.

Contains Jewelle Gomez's essay "Lorraine Hansberry: Uncommon Warrior" and Gates's essay "Our Lady: Sonia Sanchez and the Writing of a Black Renaissance."

B24.   Gavin, Christy. *American Women Playwrights 1964-1989: A Research Guide and Annotated Bibliography*. New York: Garland, 1993.

Provides production and publication information on selected plays by twenty-one African American playwrights as well as information on biographical profiles of the dramatists and criticism and reviews of the dramas. Consult the "African-American Playwrights" index for specific playwrights.

B25.   Harris, Trudier, ed. *Dictionary of Literary Biography*. Vol. 11. Detroit: Gale Research, 1985.

Includes biographical sketch and playwright profile of Sonia Sanchez. However, this sketch highlights Sanchez primarily as a poet.

B26.   Harrison, Paul Carter. *The Drama of Nommo*. New York: Grove Press, 1972.

Centered around the "Africanness" in American black life, particularly how it is expressed in African American drama. Consult the index for brief references to Alice Childress, Adrienne Kennedy, Lorraine Hansberry, and Sonia Sanchez.

B27.   Hart, Lynda, ed. *Making a Spectacle: Feminist Essays on Contemporary Women's Theatre*. Ann Arbor: Univ. of Michigan Press, 1989.

Includes Margaret Wilkerson's essay entitled "Music as Metaphor: New Plays of Black Women" where Wilkerson examines the plays of Ntozake Shange, Alexis DeVeaux, Alice Childress, P.J. Gibson, and Aishah Rahman; and Mary DeShazer's "Rejecting Necrophilia: Ntozake Shange and the Warrior Re-Revisioned" where DeShazer examines the drama of Shange.

B28.   Haskins, James. *Black Theater in America*. New York: Thomas Crowell, 1982.

Contains nine chapters on black theater which briefly mention Lorraine Hansberry and Ntozake Shange. Consult the index for specific references to these playwrights.

B29.   Hatch, James V. *Black Image on the American Stage: A Bibliography of Plays and Musicals, 1770-1970*. New York: DBS Publications, 1970.

Provides bibliographic information on African American dramas and musicals from 1770-1970. Consult the index for entries on individual contemporary female dramatists.

B30.   Hatch, James V., and Omanii Abdullah. *Black Playwrights, 1823-1977: An Annotated Bibliography*. New York: Bowker, 1977.

Provides extensively annotated bibliographic information on dramas by African Americans from 1823-1977. Consult the index for entries on individual contemporary female dramatists.

B31.   Hay, Samuel. *African American Theatre: An Historical and Critical Analysis*. Cambridge: Cambridge University Press, 1994.

Outlines the schools of African American drama in several essays and includes references to contemporary playwrights like Alice Childress, Pearl Cleage, Adrienne Kennedy, and Ntozake Shange. Consult the index for specific references.

B32.   Hull, Gloria, P.B. Scott, and Barbara Smith, eds. *But Some of Us Are Brave: Black Women's Studies*. Old Westbury, NY: Feminist Press, 1982.

Includes Jeanne-Marie Miller's essay entitled "Black Women Playwrights from Grimké to Shange" which examines the works of Martie Charles, Alice Childress, Lorraine Hansberry, Adrienne Kennedy, Sonia Sanchez, and Ntozake Shange.

B33.   King, Woodie, Jr. *Black Theatre: Present Condition*. New York: Publishing Center for Cultural Resources, 1981.

Contains a collection of essays and interviews pertaining to black theatre. King pays limited attention to contemporary African American female playwrights; however, he does make mention of Shange's *for colored girls* in several chapters, and he includes the essay "Legacy of *A Raisin in the Sun*: Hansberry's Children" in his collection.

B34.   Kolin, Philip C. *American Playwrights Since 1945: A Guide to Scholarship, Criticism, and Performances*. Westport, CT: Greenwood, 1989.

Contains an assessment of forty playwrights, two of whom are Lorraine Hansberry and Ntozake Shange. Sections are divided as follows: playwrights' reputation, primary bibliography for their works, a listing of essays and interviews, production history for the dramas, and a survey of secondary sources for these playwrights.

B35.   Lewis, Allan. *American Plays and Playwrights of the Contemporary Theatre*. New York: Crown, 1965; rev. ed. 1970.

Makes brief reference to Alice Childress and Lorraine Hansberry in the chapter "Trends of the Decade."

B36.   Lewis, Emory. *Stages: The Fifty-Year Childhood of the American Theatre*. Englewood Cliffs, NJ: Prentice-Hall, 1969.

Assesses the importance of Hansberry's *A Raisin in the Sun* and *The Sign in Sidney Brustein's Window* to African American drama as it is represented in the American theatre. Consult the index for other brief references to Hansberry and to Alice Childress.

B37.   MacNicholas, John. *Dictionary of Literary Biography: Twentieth-Century American Dramatists*. Vol. 7. Part 1. Detroit: Gale Research, 1981.

Contains biographic and bibliographic information about Alice Childress and Lorraine Hansberry and their dramas.

B38.   Magill, Frank, ed. *Critical Survey of Drama: Supplement*. Pasadena: Salem Press, 1987.

Contains profiles about authors of contemporary drama. Consult the alphabetical index for entries of contemporary African American female playwrights.

B39.   ———. *Great Women Writers: The Lives and Works of 135 of the World's Most Important Women Writers, From Antiquity to the Present*. New York: Holt & Co., 1994.

Cites the principal forms or genres of writers and their representative works, the achievements of the writers, a biographical analysis of the writer, and a brief bibliography of the works of the writers. Contemporary African American female playwrights featured are Lorraine Hansberry, Adrienne Kennedy, and Ntozake Shange.

B40.   Metzger, Linda, et al., eds. *Black Writers: A Selection of Sketches from Contemporary Authors*. Detroit: Gale Research, 1989.

Includes biographical information and general comments of the plays of Vinnette Carroll, Alice Childress, J. California Cooper, Alexis De Veaux, Rita Dove, J.E. Franklin, Adrienne Kennedy, Sonia Sanchez, and Ntozake Shange.

B41.   Mitchell, Loften. *Black Drama: The Story of the American Negro in the Theatre*. New York: Hawthorn Books, 1967.

Includes twelve essays on the drama of the Negro. The essay that addresses Alice Childress, Lorraine Hansberry, and Adrienne Kennedy is entitled "The Nineteen-Sixties: Broadway Reconsidered." The index also provides a guide to other brief mentions of these playwrights.

B42.   Olauson, Judith. *American Women Playwrights: A View of Criticism and Characterization*. Troy, NY: Whitson, 1981.

Examines American women playwrights from 1930-1970. Consult the index for specific references to Lorraine Hansberry and Adrienne Kennedy.

B43.   Peterson, Bernard L. *Contemporary Black American Playwrights and Their Plays: A Biographical Directory and Dramatic Index*. Westport, CT: Greenwood Press, 1988.

Provides extensively annotated biographic and bibliographic information on contemporary African American playwrights and their plays; provides summaries of their published and produced plays; and includes production information where available.

B44.   Robinson, Alice, Vera M. Roberts, and Milly Barranger. *Notable Women in American Theatre: A Biographical Dictionary*. Westport, CT: Greenwood, 1989.

Provides a biographical dictionary of over fifty women in American theatre, five of whom are Vinnette Carroll, Alice Childress, Lorraine Hansberry, Adrienne Kennedy, and Ntozake Shange.

B45.   Rush, Theresa, Carol F. Meyers, and Esther Arata. *Black American Writers Past and Present: A Biographical and Bibliographical Dictionary*. 2 vols. Metuchen, NJ: Scarecrow Press, 1975.

Provides biographical and bibliographical information for African American writers. Consult the alphabetical index for individual playwrights.

B46.   Ryan, Bryan, ed. *Major Twentieth Century Writers: A Selection of Sketches from Contemporary Authors*. 4 vols. Detroit: Gale Research, 1991.

Examines a selection of the works of the following contemporary African American female playwrights: Alice Childress, Lorraine Hansberry, Gayl Jones, and Ntozake Shange. Consult the cumulative drama index in volume four for other references.

B47.   Salem, James. *A Guide to Critical Reviews, Part I: American Drama, 1909-1982.* 3rd ed. Metuchen, NJ: Scarecrow Press, 1984.

Provides sources for critical reviews of dramas. Consult the alphabetically listed index of titles and of authors for specific references.

B48.   Schlueter, June, ed. *Modern American Drama: The Female Canon.* Rutherford, NJ: Fairleigh Dickinson University Press, 1990.

Contains twenty-two essays on drama by female playwrights, four of which are: "Lorraine Hansberry and the Great Black Way" by Leonard Ashley, "No Place But the Funnyhouse: The Struggle for Identity in Three Adrienne Kennedy Plays" by Susan Meigs, "Whose Name, Whose Protection: Reading Alice Childress's *The Wedding Band*" by Catherine Wiley, and "'The Poetry of a Moment': Politics and the Open Form in the Drama of Ntozake Shange" by John Timpane.

B49.   Simon, John. *Uneasy Stages: A Chronicle of the New York Theatre, 1963- 1973.* New York: Random House, 1975.

Provides sources for critical reviews of dramas. Consult the alphabetically listed index of titles and of authors for specific references.

B50.   Smith, Jessie C., ed. *Epic Lives: One Hundred Black Women Who Made a Difference.* Detroit: Visible Ink Press; New York: Macmillan; Toronto: Maxwell Macmillan of Canada, 1993.

Contains biographical profiles of Lorraine Hansberry and Ntozake Shange.

B51.   ———, ed. *Notable American Black Women.* Detroit: Gale Research, 1992.

Contains profiles on the following contemporary playwrights: Alice Childress, Sarah Fabio, J.E. Franklin, Lorraine Hansberry, Abbey Lincoln, Beah Richards, and Sonia Sanchez.

B52.   Smith, Valerie, Lea Baechler, and A. Walton, eds. *African American Writers.* New York: Collier Books, 1993.

Contains biographical profiles and an examination of the works of Lorraine Hansberry, Gayl Jones, and Ntozake Shange.

B53.   Tate, Claudia. *Black Women Writers at Work.* New York: Continuum, 1983.

Includes interviews with the following contemporary female playwrights: Alexis DeVeaux, Gayl Jones, Sonia Sanchez, and Ntozake Shange.

B54.   Williams, Mance. *Black Theatre in the 1960s and 1970s: A Historical-Critical Analysis of the Movement.* Westport, CT: Greenwood Press, 1985.

Contains six chapters which highlight the black theatre of the 60s and 70s. Limited attention is given female playwrights; thus, readers should consult the index to find any brief mention of contemporary female playwrights Vinnette Carroll, Alice Childress, Micki Grant, Lorraine Hansberry, Adrienne Kennedy, Judi Ann Mason, Sonia Sanchez, and Ntozake Shange.

B55.   Woll, Allen. *Dictionary of Black Theatre: Broadway, Off-Broadway, and Selected Harlem Theatres.* Westport, CT: Greenwood Press, 1983.

Includes, according to the preface, "references to Broadway, Off-Broadway, and Selected Harlem plays that are by, about, with, for, and related to blacks from 1898 to 1981." Specific references to individual dramatists or dramas may be found by consulting either the playwright index, the plays and films index, or the song index.

III INDIVIDUAL DRAMATISTS

The following playwrights have had at least one drama published since 1959. For those playwrights with multiple published works, the dramas are listed chronologically.

C1.   **ABRAMSON, DOLORES**

C1.1.   ———. *The Light. Three Hundred and Sixty Degrees of Blackness Comin' at You.* Ed. Sonia Sanchez. New York: 5X Publishing, 1971. n. pag.

The one-act drama examines the proper behavior of black women as seen by God and by the devil.

Secondary Sources
Scholarly Criticism
Peterson, Bernard L. "Abramson, Dolores." *Contemporary Black American Playwrights.* Westport, CT: Greenwood, 1988.

C2.   **AHMAD, DOROTHY**

C2.1.   ———. "Papa's Daughter." *The Drama Review* (Black Theatre Issue) 12 (Summer 1968): 139-145.

The one-act drama, according to *CBAP*, "explores the unwholesome relationship that has developed between a father and daughter after the death of the mother, and the daughter's attempt to cope with this problem" (4).

Secondary Sources

Scholarly Criticism

Peterson, Bernard L. "Ahmad, Dorothy." *Contemporary Black American Playwrights*. Westport, CT: Greenwood, 1988.

C3.   **ANDERSON, T. DIANNE**

C3.1.   ———. *Come Yesterday. The Unicorn Died at Dawn: Plays, Poems, Songs and Other Writings*. Dianne Anderson. Lutz, FL: Anderson Publishing, 1981. n. pag.

A one-act drama that examines a young black man's search for faith.

C3.2.   ———. *Just Friendly*. Anderson n. pag.

A one-act drama that reflects the reenactment of the trial by a lawyer and a defendant after he has been tried and acquitted.

C3.3.   ———. *Nightcap*. Anderson n. pag.

A one-act drama that reflects a man's attempt to seduce the woman with whom he is having a nightcap.

C3.4.   ———. *Home to Roost*. Anderson n. pag.

A three-act drama that examines how a mother's return home after several years of absence creates turmoil and difficulty in the lives of the men at home.

C3.5.   ———. *Closing Time*. Anderson n. pag.

A comedy-skit that reflects the experience of a woman who insists on buying only one shoe just before the shoe store is about to close for the day.

C3.6.   ———. *The Unicorn Died at Dawn*. Anderson n. pag.

The two-act drama examines the effects of racism and black awareness in the lives of a black middle-class family.

C3.7.   ———. *Black Sparrow*. Anderson n. pag.

A full-length drama that examines the life of a black Vietnam veteran.

C3.8.   ———. *Cryo*. Anderson n. pag.

The one-act drama examines the playwright's experience of having a cryothalamectomy.

C3.9.   ———. *The Gift of Harmonia.* Anderson n. pag.

A two-act drama that examines the life of a musician who will do anything to gain a commission, including sacrificing his principles.

Secondary Sources
Scholarly Criticism
Peterson, Bernard L. "Anderson, T. Dianne." *Contemporary Black American Playwrights.* Westport, CT: Greenwood, 1985.

C4.   BATSON, SUSAN

C4.1.   ———.   *Hoodoo Talkin.   Three Hundred and Sixty Degrees of Blackness.* Ed. Sonia Sanchez. New York: 5X Publishing, 1971. n. pag.

The one-act drama details a discussion of the black experience as seen by four black women.

Secondary Sources
Scholarly Criticism
Peterson, Bernard L. "Batson, Susan." *Contemporary Black American Playwrights.* Westport, CT: Greenwood, 1985.

C5.   BEASLEY, ELOIS

C5.1.   ———. *The Fallen Angel. New Plays for the Black Theatre.* Ed. Woodie King, Jr. Chicago: Third World Press, 1989. 17-36.

A one-act drama that examines a woman's struggle with infidelity after finding out that her husband is gay.

C6.   BOOKER, SUE

C6.1.   ———. *The Flags. Cry at Birth.* Ed. Merrel D. Booker, Sr. et al. New York: McGraw-Hill, 1971. 139-143.

A one-act drama that examines the life of a black woman whose only income is selling Confederate flags. Eventually, she is convinced by a white civil rights worker to stop selling the flags.

Secondary Sources

Scholarly Criticism

Peterson, Bernard L. "Booker, Sue." *Contemporary Black American Play-wrights.* Westport, CT: Greenwood, 1985.

C7.   BROWN, BEVERLY

C7.1.   ———. "The Snake Chief." *Negro History Bulletin* March 1971: 70-71.

A one-act drama that examines South African myths and legends.

Secondary Sources

Scholarly Criticism

Peterson, Bernard L. "Brown, Beverly." *Contemporary Black American Playwrights.* Westport, CT: Greenwood, 1985.

C8.   BROWN-GUILLORY, ELIZABETH

C8.1.   ———. *Mam Phyllis.* *Wines in the Wilderness: Plays by African American Women From the Harlem Renaissance to the Present.* Ed. Elizabeth Brown-Guillory. Westport, CT: Greenwood, 1990. 191-227.

The three-act drama examines the distinctive aspects of southern Louisiana life while addressing the universal issues of aging, religion, love, and ambition.

C8.2.   ———. *Snapshots of Broken Dolls.* Colorado Springs, CO: Contemporary Drama Service, 1987.

A one-act drama that examines the lives of three generations of Louisiana women as they wait for the birth of the fourth generation child. All of the women from the different generations symbolically give birth to their fears as the expectant mother gives birth to the fourth generation child.

Secondary Sources

Scholarly Criticism

Bryan, Violet H. "Evocations of Place and Culture in the Works of Four Contemporary Black Louisiana Writers: Brenda Osbey, Sybil Kein, Elizabeth Brown-Guillory, and Pinkie Gordon Lane." *Louisiana Literature* 4 (Fall 1987): 49-60.

Peterson, Bernard L. "Brown-Guillory, Elizabeth." *Contemporary Black American Playwrights.* Westport, CT: Greenwood, 1985.

C9.   **CARLOS, LAURIE**

C9.1.   ———. *White Chocolate for My Father*. *Moon Marked and Touched by Sun*. Ed. Sydné Mahone. New York: Theatre Communications Group, 1994. 7-31.

The theatre piece explores "the multi-generational devastation of rape; rooted in the uncomplicated language of a twelve-year-old girl" (Mahone xxix).

Secondary Sources
General Articles
Southgate, Martha. "Star Quality." *Essence* Jan. 1989: 26.

C10.   **CARROLL, VINNETTE**

C10.1.   ———. (With Micki Grant) *Don't Bother Me, I Can't Cope*. New York: Samuel French, 1972.

A two-act musical drama "which deals with the black (and universal) problem of coping with life, utilizing songs and dances based on blues, gospel, jazz, rock, calypso, and traditional ballad rhythms" (*CBAP* 203).

C10.2.   ———. (Music and lyrics by Micki Grant) *Croesus and the Witch*. New York: Broadway Music Publishing, 1984.

The full-length musical is based on the fable of Croesus.

Secondary Sources
General Articles
"Black Women 'Star' Behind the Scenes in New York Drama: Talented Directors, Producers, Playwrights Work 'On' and 'Off' Broadway." *Ebony* April 1973: 106-108, 110-111.

Mason, Clifford. "Vinnette Carroll Is Still There Swinging." *New York Times* 19 Dec. 1976, sec. 2: 4.

Scholarly Criticism
Coven, Brenda. "Vinnette Carroll." *American Women Dramatists of the Twentieth Century: A Bibliography*. Metuchen, NJ: Scarecrow, 1982.

Fabre, Genevieve. *Drumbeats, Masks and Metaphors: Contemporary Afro-American Theatre*. Cambridge: Harvard University Press, 1983.

Peterson, Bernard L. "Carroll, Vinnette." *Contemporary Black American Playwrights and Their Plays*. Westport, CT: Greenwood, 1988.

Robinson, Alice, Vera M. Roberts, and Milly Barranger. "Vinnette Carroll." *Notable Women in American Theatre: A Biographical Dictionary*. Westport, CT: Greenwood, 1989.

Smith, Karen L. "Vinnette Carroll: Portrait of an Artist in Motion." Diss. Univ. of California, Los Angeles, 1975.

Vedder, Polly A. "Carroll, Vinnette." *Black Writers: A Selection of Sketches From Contemporary Authors*. Detroit: Gale Research, 1989.

Williams, Mance. *Black Theatre in the 1960s and 1970s*. Westport, CT: Greenwood, 1985.

C11.   **CHARLES, MARTIE**

C11.1.   ———. *Job Security*. *Black Theater USA: Forty-Five Plays by Black Americans 1847-1974*. Ed. James V. Hatch. New York: The Free Press, 1974. 766-771.

This one-act drama reflects the revenge of a young black girl whose intelligence is ignored by her teachers to insure their job security.

C11.2.   ———. *Black Cycle*. *Black Drama Anthology*. Ed. Woodie King, Jr. and Ron Milner. New York: Penguin Group, 1971. 525-552.

A two-act drama that examines the relationship of a mother and a daughter when the mother suffers from an inability to accept her blackness.

Secondary Sources
Scholarly Criticism
Brown-Guillory, Elizabeth. "Six Female Black Playwrights: Images of Blacks in Plays by Lorraine Hansberry, Alice Childress, Sonia Sanchez, Barbara Molette, Martie Charles, and Ntozake Shange." *DAI* 41/07 (1980): 3104A. Florida State Univ.

Miller, Jeanne-Marie A. "Black Women Playwrights from Grimké to Shange: Selected Synopses of Their Works." *But Some of Us Are Brave: Black Women's Studies*. Ed. Gloria T. Hull, P.B. Scott, and Barbara Smith. Old Westbury, NY: Feminist Press, 1982. 280-290.

Peterson, Bernard L. "Charles, Martie." *Contemporary Black American Playwrights and Their Plays*. Westport, CT: Greenwood, 1988.

C12. CHILDRESS, ALICE

C12.1. ———. *Wine in the Wilderness*. New York: Dramatists Play Service, 1969. Rpt. New York: Chilton Book Co., 1972. Rpt. *Wines in the Wilderness: Plays by African American Women from the Harlem Renaissance to the Present*. Ed. Elizabeth Brown-Guillory. Westport, CT: Greenwood, 1990. 1 22-149; *Black Theater USA*. Ed. James Hatch. New York: The Free Press, 1974. 738-755; *Plays by and about Women*. Ed. Victoria Sullivan and James Hatch. New York: Random House, 1973. 377-421.

A one-act drama that examines the relationship between a middle-class black artist and a street woman whom he chooses to be a model.

C12.2. ———. *The African Garden*. Excerpt in *Black Scenes*. Ed. Alice Childress. Garden City, NY: 1971. 137-145.

The musical drama examines the black man's quest for and acceptance of his African heritage.

C12.3. ———. *String*. *Mojo and String*. Alice Childress. New York: Dramatists Play Service, 1971. 25-49.

A one-act drama signifies on Guy de Maupassant's short story "A Piece of String." According to *CBAP*, "a raggedy black character who, in the tradition of a true Rastafarian, honorably survives on the discards of others, is falsely accused by middle-class blacks of stealing a wallet" (107).

C12.4. ———. *Mojo*. *Mojo and String*. Childress. New York: Dramatists Play Service, 1971. 5-23. Rpt. New York: Crown Publishers, 1973. Rpt. in The *Best Short Plays of World Theatre, 1968-73*. Ed. Stanley Richards. Philadelphia: Chilton 1970. 126-137.

A drama that examines the love of a Harlem couple after they have separated and divorced because of what they thought were irreconcilable differences.

C12.5. ———. *The Wedding Band*. New York: Samuel French, 1973. Rpt. in *The New Women's Theatre: Ten Plays by Contemporary American*

Women. Ed. Honor Moore. New York: Vintage Books, 1977. 255-338;
Nine Plays by Black Women. Ed. Margaret Wilkerson. New York:
Penguin Books, 1986. 73-133.

A two-act drama that explores the ramifications of interracial love in the
segregated South and which also explores the ramifications of patriarchal
dominance on the drama's female characters.

C12.6.   ———. *When the Rattlesnake Sounds*. New York: Coward, McCann &
Geoghegan, 1975.

The one-act drama portrays Harriet Tubman as a laundress and
abolitionist still fighting for the anti-slavery cause.

C12.7.   ———. *Let's Hear It for the Queen*. New York: Coward, McCann &
Geoghegan, 1976.

The one-act drama is, according to *CBAP* "a continuation of the Mother
Goose story about 'the Knave of Hearts who stole some tarts.'"

Primary Works Related to Drama
———. "Negro Women in Literature." *Freedomways* 6 (Winter 1966):
14-19.

———. "Why Talk About That?" *Negro Digest* 16 (Apr. 1967): 17-21.

———. "But I Do My Thing." *New York Times* 2 Feb. 1969, sec. 2:
D9.

Secondary Sources
General Articles
Downey, Maureen. "Alice Childress: Blacks Must Write About All
Issues." *Atlanta Constitution* 27 March 1986, sec. C:12.

Michaelson, Judith. "Women Playwrights and Their Stony Road." *Los
Angeles Times* 6 Nov. 1988: 47, 55-55.

"Near Broadway Playwrights." *Ebony* April 1959: 100.

Scholarly Criticism
"Alice Childress." *Black American Women Poets and Dramatists*. Ed.
Harold Bloom. New York: Chelsea House, 1996. 32–44.

Anderson, Mary Louise. "Black Matriarchy: Portrayal of Women in
Three Plays." *Negro American Literature Forum* 10 (Spring 1976):
93-95.

Austin, Gayle. "Contemporary Black Women Playwrights: A View from the Other Half." *Helicon Nine* 14-15 (Summer 1986): 120-127.

———. "Alice Childress: A Pioneering Spirit." *Sage: A Scholarly Journal on Black Women* 4 (Spring 1987): 66-68.

———. "Alice Childress: Black Woman Playwright as Feminist Critic." *Southern Quarterly* 25 (Spring 1987): 53-62.

———. "Black Women Playwrights: Exorcising Myths." *Phylon* 68 (Fall 1987): 230-238.

Betsko, Kathleen, and Rachel Koenig. "Alice Childress." *Interviews with Contemporary Women Playwrights*. New York: Beach Tree Books, 1987. 62-74.

Brown, Elizabeth Barnsley. "Shackles on a Writer's Pen: Dialogism in Plays by Alice Childress, Lorraine Hansberry, Adrienne Kennedy, and Ntozake Shange." *DAI* 57/05 (1996): 2035A. University of North Carolina.

Brown-Guillory, Elizabeth. "Alice Childress: A Pioneering Spirit." *SAGE* 4 (Spring 1987): 66–68.

———. "Black Women Playwrights: Exorcising Myths." *Phylon* 48 (Fall 1987): 229–239.

———. *Their Place on the Stage: Black Women Playwrights in America*. Westport, CT: Greenwood, 1988.

Case, Sue-Ellen. *Feminism and Theatre*. New York: Methuen, 1988.

"Childress, Alice." *Black Writers: A Selection of Sketches from Contemporary Authors*. Detroit: Gale Research, 1989.

"Childress, Alice." *Major Twentieth Century Writers: A Selection of Sketches from Contemporary Authors*. Detroit: Gale Research, 1991.

"Conversation with Alice Childress and Toni Morrison." *Conversations with Toni Morrison*. Ed. Danille Taylor-Guthrie. Jackson: UP of Mississippi, 1994. 3–9.

Coven, Brenda. "Alice Childress." *American Women Dramatists of the Twentieth Century: A Bibliography*. Metuchen, NJ: Scarecrow, 1982.

Curb, Rosemary. "An Unfashionable Tragedy of American Racism: Alice Childress's *The Wedding Band.*" *Melus* 7 (Winter 1980): 57-68.

―――. "Alice Childress." *Dictionary of Literary Biography.* Vol. 7. Ed. John MacNicholas. Detroit: Gale Research, 1981.

Dillon, John. "Alice Childress' *The Wedding Band* at the Milwaukee Repertory Theater: A Photo Essay." *Studies in American Drama 1945-Present* 4 (1989): 129-141.

Fabre, Genevieve. "Alice Childress." *Afro-American Poetry and Drama, 1760-1975: A Guide to Information Sources.* Detroit: Gale Research Co., 1979.

―――. *Drumbeats, Masks and Metaphor: Contemporary Afro-American Theatre.* Cambridge: Harvard Univ. Press, 1983.

Harris, Trudier. "Alice Childress." *Dictionary of Literary Biography.* Vol. 38. Detroit: Gale Research, 1985.

Hay, Samuel A. "Alice Childress's Dramatic Structure." *Black Women Writers, (1950-1980): A Critical Evaluation.* Ed. Mari Evans. Garden City, NY: Anchor Books, 1984. 117-128.

―――. *African American Theatre: An Historical and Critical Analysis.* Cambridge: Cambridge University Press, 1994.

Holliday, Polly. "I Remember Alice Childress." *Southern Quarterly* 25 (Spring 1987): 63-65.

Jordan, Shirley M. "Alice Childress." *Broken Silences: Interviews with Black and White Women Writers.* New Brunswick, NJ: Rutgers Univ. Press, 1993. 28-37.

Killens, John O. "The Literary Genius of Alice Childress." *Black Women Writers, (1950-1980): A Critical Evaluation.* Ed. Mari Evans. Garden City, NY: Anchor Books, 1984. 129-133.

Lewis, Allan. "Trends of the Decade." *American Plays and Playwrights of the Contemporary Theatre.* New York: Crown, 1965; rev. ed. 1970. 243- 257.

Maguire, Roberta. "Alice Childress." *The Playwright's Art: Conversations with Contemporary American Dramatists.* Ed. Jackson Bryer. New

Brunswick, NJ: Rutgers UP, 1995. 48–69.

Mason, Louise C. "The Fight to Be an American Woman and a Playwright: A Critical History from 1773 to the Present." Diss. Univ. of California, Berkeley, 1983.

Miller, Jeanne-Marie A. "Black Women Playwrights from Grimké to Shange: Selected Synopses of Their Works." *But Some of Us Are Brave: Black Women's Studies.* Ed. Gloria T. Hull, P.B. Scott, and Barbara Smith. Old Westbury, NY: Feminist Press, 1982. 280-290.

————. "Images of Black Women in Plays by Black Playwrights." *CLA Journal* 20 (June 1977): 494-507. Rpt. as "Black Women in Plays by Black Playwrights." *Women in American Theatre.* Ed. Helen Chinoy and Linda Jenkins. New York: Theatre Communications Group, 1987. 254-259.

Mitchell, Loften. "Three Writers and a Dream." *Crisis* April 1965: 219-223.

————. "The 1960s: Broadway Reconsidered." *Black Drama: The Story of the American Negro in the Theatre.* New York: Hawthorn Books, 1967. 182- 224.

Molette, Barbara. "They Speak: Who Listens?" *Black World* 25 (Apr. 1976): 28-34.

Moore, Honor. Introduction. *The New Women's Theatre: Ten Plays by Contemporary American Women.* By Moore. New York: Vintage Books, 1977. xi-xxxvi.

Peterson, Bernard L. "Childress, Alice." *Contemporary Black American Playwrights.* Westport, CT: Greenwood, 1988.

Price-Hendricks, Margo Jennett. "The Roaring Girls: A Study of Seventeenth-Century Feminism and the Development of Feminist Drama." *DAI* 48/10 (1987): 2492. U of California, Riverside.

Robinson, Alice M., Vera M. Roberts, and Milly S. Barranger. "Alice Childress." *Notable Women in the American Theatre: A Biographical Dictionary.* Westport, CT: Greenwood, 1989.

Schroeder, Patricia R. "Re-Reading Alice Childress." *Staging Difference: Cultural Pluralism in American Theatre and Drama.* Ed. Marc

Maufort. New York: Peter Lang, 1995. 323–335.

Shinn, Thelma J. "Living the Answer: The Emergence of African American Feminist Drama." *Studies in the Humanities* 17 (Dec. 1990): 149–159.

"Six Female Black Playwrights: Images of Blacks in Plays by Lorraine Hansberry, Alice Childress, Sonia Sanchez, Barbara Molette, Martie Charles, and Ntozake Shange." *DAI* 41/07 (1980): 3104A. Florida State Univ.

Smith, Jessie C, ed. "Alice Childress." *Notable Black American Women*. Detroit: Gale Research, 1992.

Turner, S.H. Regina. "Images of Black Women in the Plays of Black Female Playwrights, 1950-1975." *DAI* 43/01 (1982): 19A. Bowling Green State Univ.

Vojta, Barbara Rothman. "In Praise of African American Women: Female Images in the Plays of Alice Childress." *DAI* 54/12 (1994): 4308A. New York U.

Wiley, Catherine. "Whose Name, Whose Protection: Reading Alice Childress's *The Wedding Band*." *Modern American Drama: The Female Canon*. Ed. June Schlueter. Rutherford, NJ: Fairleigh Dickinson Univ. Press, 1990. 184-197.

Wilkerson, Margaret B. "Music as Metaphor: New Plays of Black Women." *Making a Spectacle: Feminist Essays on Contemporary Women's Theatre*. Ed. Lynda Hart. Ann Arbor: Univ. of Michigan Press, 1989. 61-75.

Williams, Mance. *Black Theatre in the 1960s and the 1970s: A Historical-Critical Analysis of The Movement*. Westport, CT: Greenwood, 1985.

Williams, V.A. "Alice Childress: An Uncompromising Playwright." *Afro-American* 14 (Oct. 1988): 4-5.

C13.   CLARK, CHINA

C13.1.   ———. "Perfection in Black." *Scripts* #7 May 1972: 4-28.

A one-act drama that examines the many conflicts that exists between African American women and men.

C13.2.   ———. *In Sorrow's Room. Neffie and In Sorrow's Room* (unverified title). China Clark. New York: Era Publishing Co., 1976. n. pag.

A three-act drama that examines the life of a woman named Sorrow who is searching for her identity despite her domineering mother and the men in her life.

C13.3.   ———. *Neffie.* Clark n. pag.

A two-act drama that explores the mythical love of an African woman for a man.

<u>Secondary Sources</u>
<u>Scholarly Criticism</u>
Peterson, Bernard L. "Clark, China (Debra)." *Contemporary Black American Playwrights.* Westport, CT: Greenwood Press, 1988.

C14.   **CLEAGE, PEARL**

C14.1.   ———. *Hospice. New Plays for the Black Theatre.* Ed. Woodie King, Jr. Chicago: Third World Press, 1989. 45-72.

A one-act drama that examines the relationship of a mother and daughter after the terminally-ill mother gives up her career as an entertainer and returns to the daughter she abandoned more than twenty years prior.

C14.2.   ———. "The Sale." *Black World* April 1973: 90.

A one-act drama that depicts a store that sells "token niggers."

C14.3.   ———. *Chain. Playwriting Women: Seven Plays from the Women's Project.* Ed. Julia Miles. Portsmouth, NY: Heinemann, 1993. 267-296.

The drama is one of the two first plays in a series of what Cleage calls her morality plays. According to Cleage's introduction to the drama, both *Chain* and *Late Bus to Mecca* "explore the vulnerability and isolation of young black women who find themselves abandoned by theAfrican-American culture, preyed upon by those who should protect them, and forced by circumstance to question the traditional values that sustained their mothers and grandmothers, but have no relevance to their own lives" ("Author's Introduction" 265).

C14.4. ———. *Late Bus to Mecca*. Miles 297-322.

The drama is one of the two first plays in a series of what Cleage calls her morality plays. According to Cleage's introduction to the drama, both *Late Bus to Mecca* and *Chain* "explore the vulnerability and isolation of young black women who find themselves abandoned by the African-American culture, preyed upon by those who should protect them, and forced by circumstance to question the traditional values that sustained their mothers and grandmothers, but have no relevance to their own lives" ("Author's Introduction" 265).

C14.5. ———. *Flyin' West*. *Black Drama in America: An Anthology*. Ed. Darwin Turner. Washington, DC: Howard University Press, 1994. 667-724.

The full-length drama "focuses on the lives of four African American women who, like many African Americans during the late 1800s, fled the racist south and headed for the Western frontier in search of prosperity, security, and autonomy" (Turner 667).

Primary Works Related to Drama
———. "Pearl Cleage." *I Know What the Red Clay Looks Like*. Ed. Rebecca Carroll. New York: Crown Publishers, 1994. 48-62.

Secondary Sources
General Articles
Washington, Elsie B. "Pearl Cleage." *Essence* Sept. 1993: 56.

Scholarly Criticism
Hay, Samuel. *African American Theatre: An Historical and Critical Analysis*. Cambridge: Cambridge University Press, 1994.

Peterson, Bernard L. "Cleage, Pearl." *Contemporary Black American Playwrights*. Westport, CT: Greenwood, 1988.

C15. **COLLINS, KATHLEEN**

C15.1. ———. *In the Midnight Hour*. *The Women's Project: The American Place Theatre*. Ed. Julia Miles. New York: Performing Arts Journal Publications & American Place Theatre, 1980. 35-83.

A full-length drama that examines the life of an upper-class black family on the brink of the civil rights movement.

C15.2.   ———.   *The Brothers.*   *Nine Plays by Black Women.*   Ed. Margaret Wilkerson. New York: Penguin Books, 1986. 297-346.

The three-act drama examines the futility of its black female characters who are preoccupied with their six brothers while showing that no matter how hard all of the characters try to escape their blackness, their lives are still strongly affected by race.

Secondary Sources
Scholarly Criticism
Peterson, Bernard L. "Collins, Kathleen." *Contemporary Black American Playwrights.* Westport, CT: Greenwood, 1988.

C16.   COOPER, JOAN "CALIFORNIA"

C16.1.   ———.   *Loners.*   *Center Stage.*   Ed. Eileen Ostrow. Oakland: Sea Urchin Press, 1981. 19-27.

A one-act drama that examines a male/female relationship where the male, Cool, is afraid to make a commitment until he realizes that he will lose his woman, Emma, and become a "loner."

Primary Works Related to Drama
———. "J. California Cooper." *I Know What the Red Clay Looks Like.* Ed. Rebecca Carroll. New York: Crown Publishers, 1994. 63-80.

Secondary Sources
General Articles
Oliver, Stephanie S. "J. California Cooper: From Paper Dolls to Paperbacks." *Essence* May 1991: 52.

Scholarly Criticism
"Cooper, Joan California." *Black Writers: A Selection of Sketches from Contemporary Authors.* Detroit: Gale Research, 1989.

Gray, Lynn. "J. California Cooper." *Family Five* 3 (Nov.-Dec. 1985): 1; 12.

Marshall, Barbara Jean. "Kitchen Table Talk: J. California Cooper's Use of Nommo-Female Binding and Transcendence." *Language and*

Literature in the African-American Imagination. Ed. Carol A. Black-shire-Belay. Westport, CT: Greenwood, 1992. 91-102.

————. "Mirroring Isis: An Afrocentric Analysis of the Works of Selected African-American Female Writers." *DAI* 54/07 (1994): 2574A. Temple U.

C17. CORTHRON, KIA

C17.1. ————. *Cage Rhythm. Moon Marked and Touched by Sun.* Ed. Sydné Mahone. New York: Theatre Communications Group, 1994. 38-83.

The twenty-scene drama explores the realities of African American women who are serving life sentences in prison.

C18. DAVIS, THULANI

C18.1. ————. *X. Moon Marked and Touched by Sun.* Ed. Sydné Mahone. New York: Theatre Communications Group, 1994. 94-142.

A three-act libretto that is a musical biography of civil rights activist Malcolm X.

Secondary Sources
General Articles
Knight, Kimberley. "Thulani Davis: Writing the Untold Stories." *Essence* May 1992: 60.

Scholarly Criticism
"Interview with Thulani Davis." *The Dispatch* 5 (Spring 1987): 10-12.

C19. DEVEAUX, ALEXIS

C19.1. ————. *The Tapestry. Nine Plays by Black Women.* Ed. Margaret Wilkerson. New York: Penguin Books, 1986. 139-195.

A two-act drama that examines the life of a black woman, Jet, as a social, political, and sexual being. She tries to balance all of these aspects of her life while maintaining her happiness.

Secondary Sources

Scholarly Criticism

"DeVeaux, Alexis." *Black Writers: A Selection of Sketches from Contemporary Authors.* Detroit: Gale Research, 1989.

Gomez, Jewelle L. "Alexis DeVeaux." *Contemporary Lesbian Writers of the United States: A Bio-Bibliographical Critical Sourcebook.* Eds. Sandra Pollack and Denise Knight. Westport, CT: Greenwood, 1993. 174–180.

Lourdes, Paul. "Alexis DeVeaux's *The Tapestry*: A Female Stance." *Literature and Politics in Twentieth Century America.* Ed. J.L. Plakkattam and Prashant Sinha. Hyderabad, India: American Studies Research Center, 1993. 50-56.

Peterson, Bernard L. "DeVeaux, Alexis." *Contemporary Black American Playwrights.* Westport, CT: Greenwood, 1988.

Ramsey, Priscilla. "Alexis DeVeaux." *Dictionary of Literary Biography.* Vol. 38. Detroit: Gale Research Co., 1985.

Shewey, Don. "Gay Theatre Grows Up." *American Theatre* 5 (May 1988): 11-17, 52-53.

Tate, Claudia. "Alexis DeVeaux." *Black Women Writers at Work.* New York: Continuum, 1983. 49-59.

Wilkerson, Margaret. "Music as Metaphor: New Plays of Black Women." *Making a Spectacle: Feminist Essays on Contemporary Women's Theatre.* Ed. Lynda Hart. Ann Arbor: Univ. of Michigan Press, 1989. 61-75.

C20. DOVE, RITA

C20.1. ———. *The Darker Face of the Earth.* Brownsville, OR: Story Line Press, 1994.

The fourteen-scene drama explores the incestuous relationship between a male slave and his female mistress. Unknowingly, the male slave kills his father and sleeps with his mother.

Secondary Sources
Scholarly Criticism
Bigelow, Barbara C., ed. "Rita Dove." *Contemporary Black Biography: Profiles from the International Black Community.* 6 vols. Detroit: Gale Research, 1994.

Jones, Kirkland C. "Rita Dove." *Dictionary of Literary Biography.* Vol. 120. Detroit: Gale Research, 1992.

"Rita Dove." *Contemporary Black Biography: Profiles from the International Black Community.* Detroit: Gale Research, 1994.

"Rita Dove." *Black American Women Poets and Dramatists.* Ed. Harold Bloom. New York: Chelsea House, 1996. 59–73.

Walsh, William. "Isn't Reality Magic? An Interview with Rita Dove." *The Kenyon Review* 16 (Summer 1994): 142-154.

C21.   FABIO, SARAH WEBSTER

C21.1.   ———. "The Saga of the Black Man." Privately printed. Distributed by Turn Over Book Store. n.d.

An eight-act revolutionary drama that depicts the lives of such historic figures as Nat Turner and Marcus Garvey and historic events like the Amistad, the slave revolt, and the Civil War.

Secondary Sources
Scholarly Criticism
Peterson, Bernard L. "Fabio, Sarah Webster." *Contemporary Black American Playwrights.* Westport, CT: Greenwood, 1988.

Smith, Jessie C., ed. "Sarah Webster Fabio." *Notable Black American Women.* Detroit: Gale Research, 1992.

C22.   FLAGG, ANN (KATHRYN)

C22.1.   ———. *Great Gettin' Up Morning.* New York: Samuel French, 1964.

A one-act drama that "concerns the experiences of a southern black family on the morning that their daughter is to enter a previously all white school" (*CBAP* 173).

Secondary Sources
Scholarly Criticism
Peterson, Bernard L. "Flagg, Ann (Kathryn)." *Contemporary Black American Playwrights*. Westport, CT: Greenwood, 1988.

C23.   **FRANKLIN, J. E.**

C23.1.   ———. *Black Girl*. New York: Dramatists Play Service, 1973; Rpt. as *Black Girl from Genesis to Revelations*. Washington, DC: Howard University Press, 1977.

A two-act autobiographical drama that examines the life of a young girl whose dreams of becoming a dancer threaten her relationship with her family.

C23.2.   ———. (Music by Micki Grant) *The Prodigal Sister*. New York: Samuel French, 1975.

The two-act musical is based on Franklin's earlier unpublished drama *Prodigal Daughter*. The plot of the drama follows that of the Prodigal Son; a pregnant young girl leaves home, experiences the trials of city life when all alone, and finally returns home.

C23.3.   ———. *Miss Honey's Young'uns*. *Black Drama in America: An Anthology*. Ed. Darwin Turner. Washington, DC: Howard Univ. Press, 1994. 615-665.

The full-length drama "tells the story of a young undergraduate's spiritual struggle with the racially charged ideology that informs the desegregation process at a southern university" (Turner 615).

Primary Works About Drama
———. "Genesis of a Playwright" and "Revelations of a Work." *Black Girl from Genesis to Revelations*. Washington, DC: Howard Univ. Press, 1977. 3-62.

Secondary Sources
General Articles
"Black Women 'Star' Behind the Scenes in New York Drama: Talented Directors, Producers, Playwrights Work 'On' and 'Off' Broadway." *Ebony* April 1973: 106-108, 110-111.

Gussow, Mel. "Women Playwrights Show New Strength." *New York Times* 15 Feb. 1981, sec. 2: 4, 24.

————. "Women Playwrights: New Voices in the Theater." *New York Times Magazine* 1 May 1983: 22-27.

————. "Women Write New Chapter." *New York Times* 8 June 1989: C3.

Hunter, Charlayne. "Black Women Combine Lives and Talent in Play." *New York Times* 13 July 1971: 19.

"9 Playwrights Win Rockefeller Grants." *New York Times* 27 Apr. 1980: 70.

"Scenes in New York Drama: Talented Directors, Producers, Playwrights Work 'On' and 'Off' Broadway." *Ebony* Apr. 1973: 107-108, 110-111.

Scholarly Criticism
Beauford, Fred. "Conversation with *Black Girl's* Franklin." *Black Creation* 3 (Fall 1971): 38-40.

Curb, Rosemary K. "'Goin' through the Changes': Mother-Daughter Confrontations in Three Recent Plays by Black Women." *Kentucky Folklore Record* 25 (1979): 96-102.

"Franklin, J.E." *Black Writers: A Selection of Sketches from Contemporary Authors*. Detroit: Gale, 1989.

Hay, Samuel. *African American Theatre: An Historical and Critical Analysis*. Cambridge: Cambridge Univ. Press, 1994.

Miller, Jeanne-Marie A. "Images of Black Women in Plays by Black Playwrights." *CLA Journal* 20 (June 1977): 494-507. Rpt. as "Black Women in Plays by Black Playwrights." *Women in American Theatre*. Ed. Helen Chinoy and Linda Jenkins. New York: Theatre Communications Group, 1987. 254- 259.

————. "Franklin, J.E." *Dictionary of Black Theatre*. Westport, CT: Greenwood, 1983. 207-208.

Parks, Carol. "J.E. Franklin, Playwright." *Black World* 21 (Apr. 1972): 49- 50.

Peterson, Bernard L. "Franklin, J.E." *Contemporary Black American Playwrights*. Westport, CT: Greenwood, 1988.

Smith, Jessie C., ed. "J.E. Franklin." *Notable Black American Women*. Detroit: Gale Research, 1992.

C24.   FREEMAN, CAROL

C24.1.   ———. *The Suicide. Black Fire*. Ed. Leroi Jones and Larry Neal. New York: William Morrow, 1968. 631-636.

The one-act drama revolves around an argument in an apartment building over a neighbor's refusal to turn down the music to show respect for the dead.

Secondary Sources

Scholarly Criticism
Peterson, Bernard L. "Freeman, Carol." *Contemporary Black American Playwrights*. Westport, CT: Greenwood, 1988.

C25.   GIBSON, P. J.

C25.1.   ———. *Brown Silk and Magenta Sunsets. Nine Plays by Black Women*. Ed. Margaret Wilkerson. New York: Penguin Books, 1986. 427-505.

The two-act drama examines the passionate and obsessive love that destroys the character Lena Salvinoni.

C25.2.   ———. *Long Time Since Yesterday*. New York: Samuel French, 1985. Rpt. in *Black Thunder*. Ed. William Branch. New York: Penguin, 1992. 211-275.

The two-act drama examines the past and present lives of five women after the suicidal death of one of their best friends.

C25.3.   ———. *Konvergence. New Plays for the Black Theatre*. Ed. Woodie King, Jr. Chicago: Third World Press, 1989. 73-96.

A one-act drama that reflects the reunion of a black couple who had separated in hopes of finding themselves. The reunion reveals that they have outgrown each other.

Secondary Sources

Scholarly Criticism

Adams, Julyette Tamy. "Keepers of the Oral Traditions: An Afrocentric Analysis of Representative Plays by African-American Females, 1970–1984." *DAI* 57/01 (1995): 0210. Bowling Green State U.

Peterson, Bernard L. "Gibson, P.J." *Contemporary Black American Playwrights*. Westport, CT: Greenwood, 1988.

Wilkerson, Margaret. "Music as Metaphor: New Plays of Black Women." *Making a Spectacle: Feminist Essays on Contemporary Women's Theatre*. Ed. Lynda Hart. Ann Arbor: Univ. of Michigan Press, 1989. 61-75.

C26. **GRANT, MICKI (MINNIE PERKINS)**

C26.1. ———. (With Vinnette Carroll) *Don't Bother Me, I Can't Cope*. New York: Samuel French, 1972.

A two-act musical drama "which deals with the black (and universal) problem of coping with life, utilizing songs and dances based on blues, gospel, jazz, rock, calypso, and traditional ballad rhythms" (*CBAP* 203).

C26.2. ———. (Book by Vinnette Carroll) *Croesus and the Witch*. New York: Broadway Music Publishing, 1984.

The full-length musical is based on the fable of Croesus.

Secondary Sources

General Articles

Flatley, Guy. "Don't Worry, Micki Can Cope." *New York Times* 7 (May 1972), sec. 2: 1, 7.

"Micki Grant." *New York Times Biographical Edition* 3 (1972): 960.

Peterson, M. "Micki Grant." *Essence* Nov. 1972: 32.

"She Can Cope." *Ebony* Feb. 1973: 100-109.

Scholarly Criticism

Coven, Brenda. "Micki Grant." *American Women Dramatists of the Twentieth Century: A Bibliography*. Metuchen, NJ: Scarecrow, 1982.

Peterson, Bernard L. "Grant, Micki." *Contemporary Black American Playwrights*. Westport, CT: Greenwood, 1988.

Williams, Mance. *Black Theatre in the 1960s and the 1970s: A Historical Analysis of the Movement*. Westport, CT: Greenwood, 1985.

C27.   HANSBERRY, LORRAINE

C27.1   ———. *A Raisin in the Sun*. New York: Random House, 1959. Rpt. in *Contemporary Black Drama*. Ed. Clinton Oliver and Stephanie Sills. New York: Charles Scribner's Sons, 1971. 27-120; *Six American Plays for Today*. Ed. Bennett Cerf. New York: Random House, 1961. 299-403; *A Raisin in the Sun* and *The Sign in Sidney Brustein's Window*. Lorraine Hansberry. New York: New American Library, 1987. 21-151; *Four Contemporary American Plays*. Ed. Bennett Cerf. New York: Vintage/Random House, 101-205; *Playreader's Repertory: An Anthology for Introduction to the Theatre*. Ed. Melvin White and Frank Whiting. Glenview, IL: Scott, Foresman,1970. 681-759; *The Art of Drama*. Ed. R.F. Dietrich, William Carpenter, and Kevin Kerrane. New York: Holt, Rinehart and Winston, 1969. 523-595; *Plays of Our Time*. Ed. Bennett Cerf. New York: Random House, 1967. 545-630; *Discovery and Recollections*. Ed. Elizabeth Heisch. New York: Holt, Rinehart and Winston, 1970. 425-488; *Afro-American Literature: Drama*. Ed. William Adams, Peter Conn, and Barry Slepian. Boston: Houghton Mifflin, 1970. 1-97; *Exploring Literature*. Ed. Lynn Altnenbernd. New York: Macmillan, 1970. 598-648; *Black Theatre: A Twentieth Century Collection of the Work of Its Best Playwrights*. Ed. Lindsay Patterson. New York: Dodd, Mead, and Co., 1971. 221-276; *Generations: An Introduction to Drama*. Ed. M.S. Barranger and Daniel Dodson. New York: Harcourt Brace Jovanovich, 1971. 5-86; *The Realities of Literature*. Ed. Richard Dietrich. Waltham, MA: Xerox College Press, 1971. 551-624; *Quartet: A Book of Stories, Plays, Poems, and Critical Essays*. Ed. Harold Simonson. New York: Harper and Row, 1973. 514-587; *Eight American Ethnic Plays*. Ed. Francis Griffith and Joseph Mersand. New York: Scribner's, 1974. 221-272; *An Introduction to Theatre and Drama*. Ed. Marshall and Pat Cassady. Skokie, IL: National Textbook, 1975. 558-617; *Two Voices: Writing about Literature*. Ed. Ken Symes. Boston: Houghton Mifflin, 1976. 139-210.

A three-act drama that examines black family life, particularly how it is affected by racism and greed.

C27.2   ———. *The Sign in Sidney Brustein's Window*. New York: Random

House, 1965; Rpt. Samuel French, 1965; Rpt. in *A Raisin in the Sun and The Sign in Sidney Brustein's Window*. Lorraine Hansberry. New York: New American Library, 1987. 208-340; *The Best American Plays, 6th Series*. Ed. John Gassner and Clive Barnes. New York: Crown, 1971. 227-275.

The three-act drama is "a story of a white, Jewish, liberal Greenwich Village intellectual, his aspiring actress wife, and their circle of bohemian and colorful friends, set against the background of a heated political campaign" (*CBAP* 225).

C27.3.   ————. *To Be Young, Gifted and Black*. Englewood Cliffs, NJ: Prentice Hall, 1969. Rpt. Signet Books/New American Library, 1970; New York: Samuel French, 1971.

The two-act drama is a kaleidoscope of Hansberry's published and unpublished works which together reflect her life as a black woman and as an artist.

C27.4.   ————. *Toussaint: Excerpt from Act I of a Work in Progress*. Excerpt in *Nine Plays by Black Women*. Ed. Margaret Wilkerson. New York: Penguin Books, 1986. 47-67.

The one-act excerpt introduces the bravery of Toussaint L'Ouverture, freedom fighter for Haiti.

C27.5.   ————. *The Drinking Gourd. Les Blancs: The Collected Last Plays of Lorraine Hansberry*. Lorraine Hansberry. New York: Random House, 1972. 163-220; *Black Theater USA*. Ed. James Hatch. New York: The Free Press, 1974. 714-736.

A three-act drama set in the 1850s that focuses on the life of a black woman during slavery. It also exposes the brutality of slavery and the resistance of blacks to the way they were treated.

C27.6.   ————. *Les Blancs*. New York: Samuel French, 1972. Rpt. *Les Blancs: The Collected Last Plays of Lorraine Hansberry*. Hansberry 37-139.

The three-scene drama examines the problem of color and colonialism in the world while exploring the role of color in these conflicts.

C27.7.   ————. *What Use Are Flowers? Les Blancs: The Collected Last Plays of Lorraine Hansberry*. Hansberry 228-261.

The drama examines the life of a hermit after civilization has been destroyed by an atomic holocaust. Since the only people who survive are children, the hermit is left to teach them the ways of the old society, including "the use of the flowers."

Primary Works About Drama
————. "Willy Loman, Walter Younger, and He Who Must Live." *Women in Theatre: Compassion and Hope*. Ed. Karen Malepede. New York: Drama Books Publishers, 1983. 166-176. Rpt. from *The Village Voice Reader*. Ed. Daniel Wolf and Edwin Francher. New York: Doubleday, 1962. n. pag.

————. "The Negro in American Theatre." *American Playwrights on Drama*. Ed. Horst Frenz. New York: Hill & Wang, 1965. 160-167.

Secondary Sources
General Articles
Bailey, Peter. "'Raisin': Lorraine Hansberry's Award Winning Play Becomes Musical Hit on Broadway." *Ebony* May 1974: 74-80.

Baraka, Amiri. "'Raisin in the Sun's' Enduring Passion." *Washington Post* 16 Nov. 1986, sec. Fl: 3. Rpt. as "A Critical Reevaluation: *A Raisin in the Sun's* Enduring Passion." *A Raisin in the Sun* and *The Sign in Sidney Brustein's Window*. Lorraine Hansberry. New York: Random House, 1965. 9- 20.

Braine, John. "An Appreciation: Sidney Brustein—A 'Great' Play—No Other Word is Possible." *A Raisin in the Sun* and *the Sign in Sidney Brustein's Window*. Lorraine Hansberry. New York: New American Library, 1987. 155-159.

Normant, Lynn. "'*Raisin*' Celebrates Its 25th Anniversary." *Ebony* March 1984: 57-60.

Pollack, Joe. "A Magnificent Revival of 'Raisin in the Sun'." *St. Louis Post-Dispatch* 10 Sept. 1984, sec. 4B: 1-2.

Robertson, Nan. "Dramatist Against Odds." *New York Times* 8 Mar. 1959, sec. 2: 3.

Rich, Frank. "An Appreciation: *A Raisin in the Sun*, the 25th Anniversary." *A Raisin in the Sun and the Sign in Sidney Brustein's Window*. Lorraine Hansberry. New York: New American Library, 1987. 7-8.

Seaton, Sandra. "A Raisin in the Sun: A Study in Afro-American Culture." *Midwestern Miscellany* 20 (1992): 40-49.

Turkel, Studs. "An Interview with Lorraine Hansberry." *WFMT Chicago Fine Arts Guide* 10 (April 1961): 8-14.

Scholarly Criticism
Abramson, Doris E. *Negro Playwrights in the American Theatre, 1925-1959.* New York: Columbia Univ. Press, 1969.

Adams, Michael. "Lorraine Hansberry." *Dictionary of Literary Biography.* Vol. 7. Part 1. Detroit: Gale Research, 1981.

Annan, Adaku Tawia. "Revolution as Theater: Revolutionary Aesthetics in the Works of Selected Black Playwrights." *DAI* 48/03 (1987): 648A. Univ. of Wisconsin, Madison.

Archer, Leonard C. *Black Images in the American Theatre.* Brooklyn: Pageant-Poseidon, 1973.

Ashley, Leonard. "Lorraine Hansberry and the Great Black Way." *Modern American Drama: The Female Canon.* Ed. June Schlueter. Rutherford, NJ: Fairleigh Dickinson Univ. Press, 1990. 151-160.

Baldwin, James. "Lorraine Hansberry at the Summit." *Freedomways* 19 (1979): 269–272.

———. "Sweet Lorraine." *To Be Young, Gifted and Black: Lorraine Hansberry in Her Own Words.* Lorraine Hansberry. New York: New American Library, 1970. xi-xv.

Barthelemy, Anthony. "Mother, Sister, Wife: A Dramatic Perspective." *The Southern Review* 21 (Summer 1985): 770–789.

Bavaria, Richard E. "A Value Analysis of Four Fathers from Secondary School Literature: Pap, Atticus, Willy, and Walter (Twain; Lee; Miller; Hansberry)." *DAI* 48/08 (1987): 1967A. University of Maryland, College Park.

Bennett, Jr., Lerone and Margaret G. Burroughs. "A Lorraine Hansberry Rap." *Freedomways* 19 (1979): 226–233.

Berrian, Brenda. "The Afro-American-West African Marriage Question: Its Literary and Historical Contexts." *African Literature Today* 15 (1987): 152–159.

Bigsby, C.W.E., ed. *Confrontation and Commitment: A Study of Contemporary American Drama, 1959-1966.* Columbia, MO: Univ. of Missouri Press, 1969.

Bond, Jean G, ed. *Lorraine Hansberry: Art of Thunder, Vision of Light. Freedomways* 19 (1979).

————. "Lorraine Hansberry: To Reclaim Her Legacy." *Freedomways* 19 (1979): 183-85.

Breitinger, Eckhard. "Lorraine Hansberry: *A Raisin in the Sun.*" *Das americanische Drama der Genewart.* Ed. Herbert Grabes. Kronberg: Athernaum, 1976. 153–168.

Brown, Elizabeth. "Six Female Black Playwrights: Images of Blacks in Plays by Lorraine Hansberry, Alice Childress, Sonia Sanchez, Barbara Molette, Martie Charles, and Ntozake Shange." *DAI* 41/07 (1981): 3104A. Florida State University.

————. "Lorraine Hansberry: The Politics of the Politics Surrounding *The Drinking Gourd.*" *Griot* 4 (Win.-Sum. 1985): 18-28.

Brown, Lloyd W. "Lorraine Hansberry as Ironist: A Reappraisal of *A Raisin in the Sun.*" *Journal of Black Studies* 4 (1974): 237–247.

Brown-Guillory, Elizabeth. "Lorraine Hansberry: The Politics of the Politics Surrounding *The Drinking Gourd.*" *Griot* (Official Journal of the Southern Conference on Afro-American Studies) 4 (Winter-Summer 1985): 18–28.

————. "Black Women Playwrights: Exorcising Myths." *Phylon* 48 (Fall 1987): 229–239.

Carter, Steven R. "The John Brown Theatre: Lorraine Hansberry's Cultural Views and Dramatic Goals." *Freedomways* 19 (1979): 186–191.

————. "Commitment Amid Complexity: Lorraine Hansberry's Life in Action." *Melus* 7 (1980): 39–53.

————. "Images of Men in Lorraine Hansberry's Writing." *Black American Literature Forum* 19 (Winter 1985): 160-162.

———. "Lorraine Hansberry." *Dictionary of Literary Biography*. Vol. 38. Detroit: Gale Research, 1985.

———. "Colonialism and Culture in Lorraine Hansberry's *Les Blancs*." *Melus* 15 (Spring 1988): 27-46.

———. "Inter-Ethnic Issue in Lorraine Hansberry's *The Sign in Sidney Brustein's Window*." *Explorations in Ethnic Studies* 11 (July 1988): 1-13.

———. "Lorraine Hansberry's Toussaint." *Black American Literature Forum* 23 (Spring 1989): 139-148.

———. *Hansberry's Drama: Commitment and Complexity*. Urbana, IL: Univ. of Illinois Press, 1991.

Case, Sue-Ellen. *Feminism and Theatre*. New York: Methuen, 1988.

Cheney, Anne. *Lorraine Hansberry*. Boston: Twayne Publishers, 1984.

Cooper, David O. "Hansberry's *A Raisin in the Sun*." *Explicator* 52 (Fall 1993): 59-61.

Coven, Brenda. "Lorraine Hansberry." *American Women Dramatists of the Twentieth Century: A Bibliography*. Metuchen, NJ: Scarecrow, 1982.

Cruse, Harold. *The Crisis of the Negro Intellectual*. New York: William Monow & Co., 1967.

Davis, Arthur P. "Lorraine Hansberry." *From the Dark Tower*. Washington, DC: Howard University Press, 1982. 203-208.

Effiong, Philip Uko. "In Search of a Model for African American Drama: The Example of Lorraine Hansberry, Amiri Baraka, and Ntozake Shange." *DAI* 55/07 (1995): 1744A. U of Wisconsin, Madison.

Elder, Lonnie, III. "Lorraine Hansberry: Social Consciousness and the Will." *Freedomways* 19 (1979): 213–218.

Fabre, Genevieve. "Lorraine Hansberry." *Afro-American Poetry and Drama, 1760-1975: A Guide to Information Sources*. Detroit: Gale Research, 1979.

———. *Drumbeats, Masks, and Metaphor: Contemporary Afro-*

American Theatre. Cambridge, MA: Harvard Univ. Press, 1983.

Farrison, W. Edward. "Lorraine Hansberry's Last Dramas." *CLA Journal* 16 (Dec. 1972): 188-197.

Friedman, Sharon P. "Feminist Concerns in the Works of Four Twentieth-Century American Women Dramatists: Susan Glaspell, Rachel Crothers, Lillian Hellman, and Lorraine Hansberry." *DAI* 39/02 (1977): 858A. New York Univ.

———. "Six Female Black Playwrights: Images of Blacks in Plays." *DAI* 41 (1980): 3104. Indiana Univ.

———. "Feminism as Theme in Twentieth Century American Women's Drama." *American Studies* 25 (Spring 1984): 69– 89.

Gassner, John. *Theatre at the Crossroads: Plays and Playwrights of the Mid-Century American Stage*. New York: Holt, Rinehart, and Winston, 1960.

Gill, Glenda. "Techniques of Teaching Lorraine Hansberry: Liberation from Boredom." *Negro American Literature Forum* 8 (1974): 226–228.

Giovanni, Nikki. "An Emotional View of Lorraine Hansberry." *Freedomways* 19 (1979): 281-282.

Gomez, Jewelle. "Lorraine Hansberry: Uncommon Warrior." *Reading Black, Reading Feminist*. Ed. Henry L. Gates, Jr. New York: Meridian, 1990. 307- 317.

Grant, Robert H. "Lorraine Hansberry: The Playwright as Warrior-Intellect." *DAI* 43/05 (1982): 1543A. Harvard Univ.

Gresham, Jewell H. "Lorraine Hansberry as Prose Stylist." *Freedomways* 19 (1979): 192-204.

Gruesser, John. "Lies That Kill: Lorraine Hansberry's Answer to *Heart of Darkness* in *Les Blancs*." *American Drama* 1 (Spring 1992): 1-14.

Guttman, Allen. "Integration and 'Black Nationalism' in the Plays of Lorraine Hansberry." *Americanisches Drama und Theater*. Eds. Alfred Weber and Siegfried Neuweiler. Gottingen: Vandenhoeck, 1975. 248–260.

Habicht, Werner. "Lorraine Hansberry: *The Sign in Sidney Brustein's Window*." *Theater and Drama in Amerika: Aspekte and Interpretation.* Eds. Edgar Lohner and Rudolph Haas. Berlin: Schmidt, 1978. 364–374.

Haley, Alex. "The Once and Future Vision of Lorraine Hansberry." *Freedomways* 19 (1979): 277-280.

"Hansberry, Lorraine." *Major Twentieth Century Writers: A Selection of Sketches from Contemporary Authors.* Detroit: Gale Research, 1991.

Hardin, Shirley H. "Reconciled and Unreconciled Strivings: A Thematic and Structural Study of the Autobiographies of Four Black Women (Angelou, Brooks, Hansberry, Hurston)." *DAI* 49/06 (1988): 1456A. Florida State Univ.

Haskins, James. *Black Theater in America.* New York: Thomas Crowell, 1982.

Hays, Peter L. "*Raisin in the Sun* and *Juno and the Paycock*." *Phylon* 33 (1972): 175-176.

Holtan, Orley I. "Sidney Brustein and the Plight of the American Intellectual." *Players: Magazine of American Theatre* 46 (1971): 222–225.

Humphries, Eugenia. "Lorraine Hansberry: The Visionary American Playwright." *DAI* 50/5 (1988): 1305A. State Univ. of New York, Stony Brook.

Kaiser, Ernest, and Robert Nemiroff. "A Lorraine Hansberry Bibliography." *Freedomways* 19 (1979): 285-304.

Keyssar, Helene. "Rites and Responsibilities: The Drama of Black American Women." *Feminine Focus: The New Women Playwrights.* Ed. Enoch Brater. Oxford: Oxford UP, 1989. 226–240.

————. "Sounding the Rumble of Dreams Deferred: Lorraine Hansberry's *A Raisin in the Sun*." *The Curtain and The Veil: Strategies in Black Drama.* New York: Burt Franklin and Co., 1981. 113-146.

Killens, John O. "Lorraine Hansberry: On Time!" *Freedomways* 19 (1979): 273-276.

King, Woodie, Jr. "Legacy of *A Raisin in The Sun*: Hansberry's Children." *Black Theatre: Present Condition*. New York: Publishing Center for Cultural Resources, 1981. 94-96.

————. "Lorraine Hansberry's Children: Black Artists and *A Raisin in the Sun*." *Freedomways* 19 (1979): 219–221.

Kirkwood, Porter, Jr. "Two Portraits of Lorraine Hansberry." *Freedomways* 18 (1978): 222-225.

Kolin, Philip C. "Lorraine Hansberry." *American Playwrights Since 1945: A Guide to Scholarship, Criticism, and Performances*. Westport, CT: Greenwood, 1989.

Lewis, Allan. "Trends of the Decade." *American Plays and Playwrights of the Contemporary Theatre*. New York: Crown Publishers, 1965. 243-257.

Lewis, Emory. *Stages: The Fifty-Year Childhood of the American Theatre*. Englewood Cliffs, NJ: Prentice-Hall, 1969.

"Lorraine Hansberry." *Contemporary Black Biography: Profiles from the International Black Community*. Detroit: Gale Research, 1994.

"Lorraine Hansberry." *Black American Women Poets and Dramatists*. Ed. Harold Bloom. New York: Chelsea House, 1996. 89–105.

Magill, Frank N. "Lorraine Hansberry." *Great Women Writers: The Lives and Works of 135 of the World's Most Important Women Writers, From Antiquity to the Present*. New York: Holt and Co., 1994.

Marre, Diana K. "Traditions and Departures: Lorraine Hansberry and Black Americans in Theatre." *DAI* 48/9 (1987): 2196A. Univ. of California, Berkeley.

Mayfield, Julian. "Lorraine Hansberry: A Woman for All Seasons." *Freedomways* 19 (1979): 263–268.

McKelly, James C. "Hymns of Sedition: Portraits of the Artist in Contemporary African-American Drama." *Arizona Quarterly* 48 (Spring 1992): 87– 107.

Miller, Jeanne-Marie A. "Images of Black Women in Plays by Black Playwrights." *CLA Journal* 20 (June 1977): 494-507. Rpt. as "Black

Women in Plays by Black Playwrights." *Women in American Theatre.* Ed. Helen Chinoy and Linda Jenkins. New York: Theatre Communications Group, 1987.

————. "'Measure Him Right': An Analysis of Lorraine Hansberry's *A Raisin in the Sun. Teaching American Ethnic Literatures: Nineteen Essays.* Ed. John R. Maitino and David R. Peck. Albuquerque: U of New Mexico P, 1996. 133–145.

Mitchell, Loften. "The 1960s: Broadway Reconsidered." *Black Drama: The Story of the American Negro in the Theatre.* New York: Hawthorne Books, 1967. 183-224.

Nemiroff, Robert. "From These Roots: Lorraine Hansberry and the South." *Southern Exposure* Sept./Oct. 1984: 32-36.

————. "The 101 'Final' Performances of Sidney Brustein: Portrait of a Play and Its Author." *A Raisin in the Sun and The Sign in Sidney Brustein's Window.* Lorraine Hansberry. New York: New American Library, 1987. 1-7.

Ness, David. "Lorraine Hansberry's *Les Blancs*: The Victory of the Man Who Must." *Freedomways* 13 (1973): 294-306.

Olauson, Judith. *The American Woman Playwright: A View of Criticism and Characterization.* Troy, NY: Whitson, 1981.

Parks, Sheri. "In My Mother's House: Black Feminist Aesthetics, Television, and *A Raisin in the Sun.*" *Theatre and Feminist Aesthetics.* Eds. Karen Laughlin and Catherine Schuler. Rutherford, NJ: Farleigh Dickinson UP, 1995. 200–228.

Peterson, Bernard L. "Hansberry, Lorraine." *Contemporary Black American Playwrights.* Westport, CT: Greenwood, 1988.

Phillips, Elizabeth C. "Command of Human Destiny as Exemplified in Two Plays: Lillian Hellman's *The Little Foxes* and Lorraine Hansberry's *A Raisin in the Sun.*" *Interpretations: Studies in Language and Literature* 4 (1972): 29–39.

Popkin, Michael, ed. "Hansberry, Lorraine." *Modern Black Writers: A Library of Literary Criticism.* New York: Frederick Ungar, 1978.

Powell, Bertie. "The Black Experience in Margaret Walker's Jubilee and Lorraine Hansberry's *The Drinking Gourd*." *CLA Journal* 21 (Dec. 1977): 304-311.

Rich, Adrienne. "The Problem with Lorraine Hansberry." *Freedomways* 19 (1979): 247–255.

Riley, Clayton. "Lorraine Hansberry: A Melody in a Different Key." *Freedomways* 19 (1979): 205–212.

Robinson, Alice M., Vera M. Roberts, and Milly Barranger, eds. "Lorraine Hansberry." *Notable Women in the American Theatre: A Biographical Dictionary*. Westport, CT: Greenwood Press, 1989.

Royals, Demetria Brendan. "The Me Lorraine Hansberry Knew." *Freedomways* 19 (1979): 261–262.

Rush, Theresa, Carol F. Meyers, and Esther Arata. "Lorraine Hansberry." *Black American Writers Past and Present: A Biographical and Bibliographical Dictionary*. 2 vols. Metuchen, NJ: Scarecrow Press, 1975.

Salem, James M. *A Guide to Critical Reviews: Part I: American Drama, 1909-1982*. 3rd. ed. Metuchen, NJ: Scarecrow Press, 1984.

Scheader, Catherine. *They Found a Way: Lorraine Hansberry*. Chicago: Children's Press, 1978.

Schiff, Ellen. *From Stereotype to Metaphor: The Jew in Contemporary Drama*. Albany, NY: State University of New York Press, 1982.

Seaton, Sandra. "*A Raisin in the Sun*: A Study in Afro-American Culture." *Midwestern Miscellany* 20 (1992): 40–49.

Shannon, Sandra G. "From Lorraine Hansberry to August Wilson: An Interview with Lloyd Richards." *Callaloo* 14 (Winter 1991): 124-135.

Shinn, Thelma J. "Living the Answer: The Emergence of African American Feminist Drama." *Studies in the Humanities* 17 (Dec. 1990): 149-159.

Shuman, R. Baird. "Lorraine Hansberry." *American Drama 1918-1960: An Annotated Bibliography*. Pasadena: Salem Press, 1992.

Simon, John. *Uneasy Stages: A Chronicle of the New York Theatre, 1963-1973.* New York: Random House, 1975.

Smith, Jessie C., ed. "Lorraine Hansberry." *Notable American Black Women.* Detroit: Gale, 1992.

————, ed. "Lorraine Hansberry." *Epic Lives: One Hundred Black Women Who Made a Difference.* Detroit: Visible Ink Press, 1993.

Smith, Valerie, Lea Baechler, and A. Walton, eds. "Lorraine Hansberry." *African American Writers.* NY: Collier Books, 1993.

Sohn, Hongeal. "Literature and Society: African-American Drama and American Race Relations (Hansberry, Lorraine and Baldwin, James)." *DAI* 54/07 (1993): 2582. U of Iowa.

Stubbs, Mary F. "Lorraine Hansberry and Lillian Hellman: A Comparison of Social and Political Issues in Their Plays and Screen Adaptations." *DAI* 51/11 (1991): 3759A. Indiana Univ.

Ward, Douglas T. "Lorraine Hansberry and the Passion of Walter Lee." *Freedomways* 19 (1979): 223-225.

Washington, J. Charles. "*A Raisin in the Sun* Revisited." *Black American Literature Forum* 22 (Spring 1988): 109-124.

Weales, Gerald. "A Gathering of Fugitives." *American Drama Since World War II.* New York: Harcourt, Brace, and World, 1962. 224-238.

————. "The Negro Revolution." *The Jumping-off Place: American Drama in the 1960's: From Broadway to Off-Off Broadway to Happenings.* New York: Macmillan, 1969. 107-151.

Wilkerson, Margaret B. "Excavating Our History: The Importance of Biographies of Women of Color." *Black American literature Forum* 24 (Spring 1990): 73–84.

————. "Lorraine Hansberry: The Complete Feminist." *Freedomways* 19 (1979): 235-245.

————. "The Sighted Eyes and Feeling Heart: Lorraine Hansberry." *Black American Literature Forum* 17 (Spring 1983): 8-13. Rpt. in *Essays on Contemporary American Drama.* Ed. Hedwig Bock and Albert Wertheim. Munich: M. Hueber, 1981. 91-104.

————. "*A Raisin in the Sun*: Anniversary of an American Classic." *Theatre Journal* 38 (Dec. 1986): 441-452.

————. "The Dark Vision of Lorraine Hansberry: Excerpts From a Literary Biography." *The Massachusetts Review* 38 (Winter 1987): 642-650.

Wilkerson, Margaret E. "Diverse Angles of Vision: Two Black Women Playwrights." *Intersecting Boundaries: The Theatre of Adrienne Kennedy*. Eds. Paul K. Bryant-Jackson and Lois More Overbeck. Minneapolis: U of Minnesota P, 1992. 58–75.

Williams, Mance. *Black Theatre in the 1960s and 1970s: A Historical Critical Analysis of the Movement*. Westport, CT: Greewood Press, 1985.

Williams, Ora. "Lorraine Hansberry." *American Women in the Arts and Social Sciences: A Bibliographic Survey*. Metuchen, NJ: Scarecrow Press, 1973.

Willis, Robert J. "Anger and the Contemporary Black Theatre." *Negro American Literature Forum* 8 (1974): 213–215.

Wood, Deborah J. "The Plays of Lorraine Hansberry: Studies in Dramatic Form." *DAI* 46/10 (1986): 2859A. Univ. of Wisconsin.

Zietlow, Edward R. "Wright to Hansberry: The Evolutions of Outlook in Four Negro Writers." *DA* 28 (1967): 701A.

C28. HOUSTON, DIANNE

C28.1. ————. *The Fisherman*. *Center Stage*. Ed. Eileen Ostrow. Oakland: Sea Urchin Press, 1981. 73-103.

A four-act drama that shows the negative effects of emotions like grief and passion when they go unheard or unanswered.

Secondary Sources
Scholarly Criticism

Peterson, Bernard L. "Houston, Dianne." *Contemporary Black American Playwrights*. Westport, CT: Greenwood, 1988.

C29.   **HUNKINS, LEE**

C29.1.   ————. *Revival. Center Stage.* Ed. Eileen Ostrow. Oakland: Sea
Urchin Press, 1981. 105-109.

The one-act drama shows how circumstances like survival can demand
the absence of racism.

Secondary Sources

Scholarly Criticism
Peterson, Bernard L. "Hunkins, Lee." *Contemporary Black American
Playwrights.* Westport, CT: Greenwood, 1988.

C30.   **JACKSON, CHERRY**

C30.1.   ————. *In the Master's House There Are Many Mansions. Center
Stage.* Ed. Eileen Ostrow. Oakland: Sea Urchin Press, 1981. 113-121.

The one-act drama focuses on the lives of two men, one who is dead and
one who is alive. According to *CBAP*, "during the course of the play, the
living and the dead exchange identities as well as clothes, and at the end
the corpse leaves the funeral parlor in the guise of the visitor, and the
visitor unwillingly assumes the place of the corpse on the embalming
table" (266).

Secondary Sources

Scholarly Criticism
Peterson, Bernard L. "Jackson, Cherry." *Contemporary Black American
Playwrights.* Westport, CT: Greenwood, 1988.

C31.   **JACKSON, ELAINE**

C31.1.   ————. *Toe Jam. Black Drama Anthology.* Ed. Woodie King, Jr. and
Ron Milner. New York: Penguin Group, 1971. 641-671.

The three-act drama examines the lives of two sisters. The elder is an
artist who is not allowed to develop her talents because her mother sees
her writing as useless and unproductive and the younger sister mistakes
lust for love.

C31.2.————. *Paper Dolls. Nine Plays by Black Women.* Ed. Margaret
Wilkerson. New York: Penguin Books, 1986. 349-423.

A two-act drama that examines the standards of beauty that are set by the American entertainment industry and the negative effects these standards have on black women.

Secondary Sources

General Articles
Harris, Jessica B. *N. Y. Amsterdam News* 29 Oct. 1977: D10.

"Rosemary Curb." *Michigan Chronicle*. 15 Oct. 1977, sec. B: 7.

Scholarly Criticism
Curb, Rosemary K. "'Goin' Through the Changes': Mother-Daughter Confrontations in Three Recent Plays by Black Women." *Kentucky Folklore Record* 25 (1979): 96-102.

Peterson, Bernard L. "Jackson, Elaine." *Contemporary Black American Playwrights*. Westport, CT: Greenwood, 1988.

C32. JACKSON, JUDITH ALEXA

C32.1. ———. *WOMBmanWARs*. *Moon Marked and Touched by Sun*. Ed. Sydné Mahone. New York: Theatre Communications Group, 1994. 153-185.

The one-act drama exposes the sexism present in the Anita Hill/Clarence Thomas hearings and the Desiree Washington/Mike Tyson rape trial as Jackson attempts to show that women have WOMBmanWARs with themselves "in just trying to be whole in this world" (Jackson qtd. in Mahone 145).

C33. JOHNSON, CHRISTINE

C33.1. ———. *Zwadi ya Africa Kwa Dunwa* (Africa's Gift to the World). Chicago: Free Black Press, 1960s.

The two-part drama made especially for young adult performances examines the contributions that Africa has made to the world.

Secondary Sources

Scholarly Criticism
Peterson, Bernard L. "Johnson, Christine." *Contemporary Black American Playwrights*. Westport, CT: Greenwood, 1988.

C34.   **JONES, GAYL**

C34.1.   ———. *Chile Woman. Schubert Playbook Series* 5 (1974).

The one-act drama relates black history to common people through musical forms such as the blues, jazz as well as other folk traditions.

C34.2.   ———. *Beyond Yourself (The Midnight Confessions) for Brother Ahh. Blacks on Paper.* Providence: Brown Univ., 1975.

A one-act drama that reflects a black man and woman trying to learn to love themselves and each other as they are observed by an older couple who had already gone through the same experience.

Secondary Sources

Scholarly Criticism

Byerman, Keith E. "Gayl Jones." *Dictionary of Literary Biography.* Vol. 33. Detroit: Gale Research Co., 1984.

Flora, Joseph M., and Robert Bain, eds. "Jones, Gayl." *Contemporary Fiction Writers of the South: A Bio-Bibliographical Source Book.* Westport, CT: Greenwood, 1993.

Peterson, Bernard L. "Jones, Gayl." *Contemporary Black American Playwrights.* Westport, CT: Greenwood, 1988.

Rowell, Charles. "An Interview with Gayl Jones." *Callaloo* 5 (Oct. 1982): 32-53.

"Jones, Gayl." *Major Twentieth Century Writers: A Selection of Sketches from Contemporary Authors.* Detroit: Gale Research, 1991.

Smith, Valerie, Lea Baechler, and A. Walton Litz, eds. "Gayl Jones." *African American Writers.* New York: Collier, 1991.

Tate, Claudia. "Gayl Jones." *Black Women Writers at Work.* New York: Continuum, 1983. 89-99.

Weixlmann, Joe. "A Gayl Jones Bibliography." *Callaloo* 7 (Win. 1984): 119- 131.

C35.   **JONES, LOLA (LOLA JONES AMIS)**

C35.1.   ———. *The Deal. Exploring the Black Experience in America.* Lola
Jones. Franklin Square, NY: F. Peters, 1976. Rpt. Baltimore: Morgan
State Univ., 1976. n. pag.

C35.2.   ———. *Helen. Three Plays.* Lola Jones. New York: Exposition Press,
1965. Rpt. as *Fatal Female Figures in Three Plays.* Baltimore: Morgan
State Univ., 1983. n. pag.

The two-act drama examines a mother's refusal to allow her 16-year-old
daughter to call her mother. The mother's refusal is a result of her own
unfortunate childhood where her brother was favored over her by their
mother.

C35.3.   ———. *The Other Side of the Wall.* Jones *Three Plays* n. pag.

The two-act drama is centered on a wife and her husband who will not
allow her to interfere with what happens on "the other side of the wall."
The husband next door beats his wife every night, but the first husband
prevents his wife from coming to the neighbor's aid.

C35.4.   ———. *The Places of Wrath.* Jones *Three Plays* n. pag.

A three-act drama that focuses on the repentance of an unfaithful
husband who has presumably caused the suicide of his daughter.

The two-act drama examines how greed leads to misfortune when two
men and two women each try to outsmart the other three.

C35.5.   ———. *The New Nigger, or Who's Afraid of William Faulkner?* Jones
Exploring the Black Experience in America. n. pag.

The two-act drama is, according to *CBAP*, "a satire on racism in
America, utilizing black and white stereotypes and a play-within-a-play
structure to answer the question, Who writes the black man's script?"
(279).

Secondary Sources
Scholarly Criticism
Peterson, Bernard L. "Jones, Lola." *Contemporary Black American
Playwrights.* Westport, CT: Greenwood, 1988.

C36.   **KAI, NUBIA**

C36.1.   ————. *Parting. New Plays for the Black Theatre*. Ed. Woodie King,
Jr. Chicago: Third World Press, 1989. 153-194.

The three-act drama explores the failing relationship of a black couple.
Throughout the drama, Sherrie tries to leave her lover, Sudan. She is
finally able to find the strength to be independent enough to leave him at
the end of the drama.

C37.   **KEIN, SYBIL**

C37.1.   ————. *Get Together. Wines in the Wilderness*. Ed. Elizabeth Brown-
Guillory. Westport, CT: Greenwood, 1990. 169-183.

The two-act drama examines the lives of two families, one black and one
white. To impress their guests, who are of different races from the
families, both families assume the roles of the opposite race, ultimately
showing that despite the obvious differences, blacks and whites are quite
similar.

Secondary Sources

Scholarly Criticism
Bryan, Violet Harrington. "Evocations of Place and Culture in the
Works of Four Contemporary Black Louisiana Writers: Brenda Osbey,
Sybil Kein, Elizabeth Brown-Guillory, and Pinkie Gordon Lane."
Louisiana Literature: A Review of Literature and Humanities 4 (Fall
1987): 49–60.

C38.   **KENNEDY, ADRIENNE**

C38.1.   ————. *The Owl Answers. Black Theater USA*. Ed. James Hatch. New
York: Holt, Rinehart, and Winston, 1970. 757-764; *Adrienne Kennedy
in One Act*. Adrienne Kennedy. Minneapolis: Univ. of Minnesota Press,
1988. 25- 45; *Cities in Bezique*. Adrienne Kennedy. New York: Samuel
French, 1969. 4-29; *New American Plays*. Vol. 2. Ed. William Hoffman. New York: Hill & Wang, 1968. 249-268; *Kuntu Drama*. Ed. Paul
Carter Harrison. New York: Grove Press, 1974. 169-190.

The one-act drama examines the life of a mulatto girl who cannot find
her place in either a black or white world.

C38.2. ————. *A Lesson in Dead Language. Adrienne Kennedy in One Act*. Minneapolis: Univ. of Minnesota Press, 1988. 47-53. *Collision Course*. Ed. Edward Parone. New York: Publisher's Co., 1967. 33-40.

A one-act drama that reflects a white dog trying to teach a class of young girls, highlighting the difficulty of their reciprocal communication.

C38.3. ————. *A Beast's Story. Cities in Bezique*. Adrienne Kennedy. New York: Samuel French, 1969. 31-42; *Kuntu Drama*. Ed. Paul Carter Harrison. New York: Grove Press, 1974. 191-201.

A one-act drama that symbolizes the sexual fears of a black woman.

C38.4. ————. *A Rat's Mass. Adrienne Kennedy in One Act*. Adrienne Kennedy. Minneapolis: Univ. of Minnesota Press, 1988. 55-65; *More Plays from Off-Off-Broadway*. Ed. Michael Smith. Indianapolis: Bobbs-Merrill, 1966. 345-357; *New Black Playwrights*. Ed. Stanley Couch. Baton Rouge, LA: Louisiana State Univ. Press, 1968. 61-69.

The one-act drama examines the struggle of "Brother and Sister Rat" to rid themselves of the white-Christian oppression that dominates their lives.

C38.5. ————. *Sun*. Kennedy *One Act* 67-77; Scripts #1 (New York Shakespeare Festival Public Theatre) November 1971: 51-55.

The one-act drama that was inspired by the death of Malcolm X is, according to *CBAP*, "about the scattering of a man's atoms into the Cosmos, after his body has been shattered into fragments" (289).

C38.6. ————. *Funnyhouse of a Negro*. New York: Samuel French, 1969. Rpt. in *Contemporary Black Drama*. Ed. Clinton Oliver and Stephanie Sills. New York: Charles Scribner's Sons, 1971. 187-205; *Black Drama: An Anthology*. Ed. William Brasmer and Dominick Consolo. Columbus: Merrill Publishing, 1970. 247-272; Kennedy *One Act* 1-23; *Anthology of the American Negro in the Theatre*. Ed. Lindsay Patterson. New York: Publisher's Co., 1967. 281-290.

C38.7. ————. *A Movie Star Has to Star in Black and White*. Kennedy *One Act* 79-103; *Word Plays 3*. Ed. Bonnie Marranca and Gautam Dasgupta. New York: Performing Arts Journal Publication, 1984. 51-68.

The three-scene drama examines the life of an aspiring writer who sees her actual self as a "bit role" in the movie of her life. Any significant events in her life are taken over by famous movies stars.

C38.8.   ———. *Electra (Euripides)*. Kennedy *One Act* 105-139.

The full-length drama is an adaptation of the classic mythological story of Electra and Orestes. Electra, with the help of her brother, kills her mother and her mother's lover to avenge the death of her father Agamemnon. A companion piece to *Orestes, Electra* is from the perspective of Electra.

C38.9.   ———. *Orestes (Euripides)*. Kennedy *One Act* 141-171.

The full-length drama is an adaptation of the classic mythological story of Orestes and Electra. Orestes, with the help of his sister, kills his mother and her lover to avenge the death of his father Agamemnon. A companion piece to *Electra, Orestes* is from the perspective of Orestes.

C38.10.   ———. *She Talks to Beethoven*. *The Alexander Plays*. Adrienne Kennedy. Minneapolis: Univ. of Minnesota Press, 1988. 3-23.

The theatre piece depicts a conversation between Kennedy's fictional character Suzanne Alexander with Ludwig Beethoven who comforts her until her revolutionary husband returns.

C38.11.   ———. *The Dramatic Circle*. Kennedy *Alexander* 81-107; *Moon Marked and Touched by Sun*. Ed. Sydné Mahone. New York: Theatre Communications Group, 1994. 192-210.

The full-length drama is, according to the author's headnote, "a dramatization of the events in the monologue 'The Film Club'."

C38.12.   ———. *The Film Club (A Monologue by Suzanne Alexander)*. Kennedy *Alexander* 65-79.

A theatre piece that examines the involvement of Kennedy's recurring fictional character Suzanne Alexander with a film club during the absence of her revolutionary husband.

C38.13.   ———. *The Ohio State Murders*. Kennedy *Alexander* 25-63.

The full-length drama explores the presence of violence in the writing of Kennedy's fictional character Suzanne Alexander. Suzanne recounts the story of how her twin daughters were murdered while she was attending Ohio State and cites these murders as the sources of the violent imagery in her work.

Primary Works About Drama
————. "A Growth of Images." *Modern Drama* 21 (Dec. 1977): 41-48.

————. *People Who Led to My Plays*. New York: Knopf, 1987.

————. "Becoming a Playwright." *American Theatre* 4 (Feb. 1988): 26-27.

Secondary Sources
General Articles
Berson, Misha. "*Funnyhouse of a Negro*: Unusual Play That Keeps Kicking." *San Francisco Chronicle* 19 June 1983: Datebook sec. 45.

"Five Important Playwrights Talk about Theatre." *Mademoiselle* 75 (Aug. 1972): 288-289.

Giddings, Paula. "Word Star." *Essence* 19 (Nov. 1988): 26.

Stein, Ruthe. "She's Got Her Own Place in the Sun." *San Francisco Chronicle* 31 Jan. 1980: 22.

"Where Are the Women Playwrights?" *New York Times* 20 May 1973, sec. 2:1, 3.

Scholarly Criticism
Abraham, Teresa Taisha. "Carnivalesque and American Women Dramatists of the Sixties (Kennedy, Terry, Drexler)." *DAI* 51/06 (1990): 2015A. State Univ. of New York, Stony Brook.

Abramson, Doris E. *Negro Playwrights in the American Theatre, 1925-1959*. New York: Columbia Univ. Press, 1969.

Adams, Julyette Tamy. "Keepers of the Oral Traditions: An Afrocentric Analysis of Representative Plays by African-American Females, 1970–1984." *DAI* 57/01 (1995): 0210. Bowling Green State U.

Asahina, Robert. "The Basic Training of American Playwrights: Theater and the Vietnam War." *Theater* 9 (1978): 30-37.

Barnett, Claudia. "'This Fundamental Challenge to Identity': Reproduction and Representation in the Drama of Adrienne Kennedy." *DAI* 55/06 (1994): 1422A. Ohio State U.

————. "Adrienne Kennedy and Shakespeare's Sister." *American Drama* 5 (Spring 1996): 44–56.

Benston, Kimberly W. "*Cities in Bezique*: Adrienne Kennedy's Expressionistic Vision." *CLA Journal* 20 (Dec. 1976): 235-244.

————. "Locating Adrienne Kennedy: Prefacing the Subject." *Intersecting Boundaries: The Theatre of Adrienne Kennedy*. Eds. Paul K. Bryant-Jackson and Lois More Overbeck. Minneapolis: U of Minnesota P, 1992. 113–130.

Betsko, Kathleen, and Rachel Koenig. "Adrienne Kennedy." *Interviews with Contemporary Women Playwrights*. New York: Beach Tree Books, 1987. 246-258.

Binder, Wolfgang. "A *Melus* Interview: Adrienne Kennedy." *Melus* 12 (Fall 1985): 99-108.

Blau, Hervert. "The American in American Gothic: The Plays of Sam Shepard and Adrienne Kennedy." *Modern Drama* 27 (Dec. 1984): 520-539.

Brown, Lorraine A. "For the Characters of Myself: Adrienne Kennedy's *Funnyhouse of a Negro*." *Negro American Literature Forum* 3 (Sept. 1975): 86-88.

Bryant-Jackson, Paul K. "Intersecting Boundaries: The Surrealist Theatre of Poet/Playwright Adrienne Kennedy." *African-American Review* 27 (Fall 1993): 495- 500.

————. "Kennedy's Travelers in the American and African Continuum." *Intersecting Boundaries: The Theatre of Adrienne Kennedy*. Eds. Paul K. Bryant-Jackson and Lois More Overbeck. Minneapolis: U of Minnesota P, 1992, 45–57.

Bryant-Jackson, Paul K., and Lois M. Overbeck, eds. *Intersecting Boundaries: The Theatre of Adrienne Kennedy*. Minneapolis: Univ. Of Minnesota, 1992.

Canning, Charlotte. "Contemporary Feminist Theatre." *American Drama*. Ed. Clive Bloom. New York: St. Martin's, 1995. 178–192.

Case, Sue-Ellen. *Feminism and Theatre*. New York: Methuen, 1988.

Cohn, Ruby. "Black on Black: Baraka, Bullins, Kennedy." *New American Dramatists, 1960-1980.* New York: Grove Press, 1982. 94-115.

Coven, Brenda. "Adrienne Kennedy." *American Women Dramatists of the Twentieth Century: A Bibliography.* Metuchen, NJ: Scarecrow, 1982.

Curb, Rosemary K. "Fragmented Selves in Adrienne Kennedy's *Funnyhouse of a Negro* and *The Owl Answers.*" *Theatre Journal* 32 (May 1980): 180-195.

————. "Re/cognition, Re/presentation, Re/creation in Woman-Conscious Drama: The Seer, The Seen, The Scene, The Obscene." *Theater Journal* 37 (Oct. 1985): 302-316.

————. "'Lesson I Bleed': Adrienne Kennedy's Blood Rites." *Women in American Theatre.* Ed. Helen K. Chinoy and Linda W. Jenkins. New York: Theatre Communications Group, 1987. 50-57.

————. "(Hetero)Sexual Terrors in Adrienne Kennedy's Early Plays." *Intersecting Boundaries: The Theatre of Adrienne Kennedy.* Eds. Paul K. Bryant-Jackson and Lois More Overbeck. Minneapolis: U of Minnesota P, 1992. 142–156.

Desmond, Elin. "Mimesis in Syncopated Time: Reading Adrienne Kennedy." *Intersecting Boundaries: The Theatre of Adrienne Kennedy.* Eds. Paul K. Bryant-Jackson and Lois More Overbeck. Minneapolis: U of Minnesota P, 1992. 131–141.

Diamond, Elin. "An Interview with Adrienne Kennedy." *Studies in American Drama 1945-Present* 4 (1989): 129-141.

————. "Mimesis, Mimicry, and the 'True Real'." *Modern Drama* 32 (1989): 58- 72.

————. "Rethinking Identification: Kennedy, Freud, Brecht." *The Kenyon Review* 44 (March 1992): 67-86.

————. "Adrienne Kennedy." *Speaking on Stage: Interviews with Contemporary American Playwrights.* Eds. Philip C. Kolin and Colby H. Kullman. Tuscaloosa: U of Alabama P, 1996. 125–137.

Dodson, Owen. "Who Has Seen the Wind? Playwrights and the Black Experience." *Black American Literature Forum* 11 (Fall 1977): 108-116.

"Dramatus Instructors: How Six Playwriting Teachers Fire up Their Students' Imaginations." *American Theatre* 6 (Jan. 1990): 22-26.

Elwood, William R. "*Mankind* and *Sun*: German-American Expressionism." *Text and Presentation* (Comparative Drama Papers) 11 (1991): 9-13.

Fabre, Genevieve. "Adrienne Kennedy." *Afro-American Poetry and Drama, 1760-1975: A Guide to Information Sources.* Detroit: Gale Research, 1979.

———. *Drumbeats, Masks, and Metaphor: Contemporary Afro-American Theatre.* Cambridge: Harvard Univ. Press, 1983.

Fletcher, Winona. "Who Put the 'Tragic' in the Tragic Mulatto?" *Women in American Theatre.* Ed. Helen K. Chinoy and Linda W. Jenkins. New York: Theatre Communications Group, 1987. 262-268.

Forte, Jeanie. "Realism, Narrative, and the Feminist Playwright—A Problem of Reception." *Modern Drama* 32 (March 1989): 115-127.

———. "Kennedy's Body Politic: The Mulatta, Menses, and the Medusa." *Intersecting Boundaries: The Theatre of Adrienne Kennedy.* Eds. Paul K. Bryant-Jackson and Lois More Overbeck. Minneapolis: U of Minnesota P, 1992. 157–169.

———. "Realism, Narrative, and the Feminist Playwright—A Problem of Reception." *Feminist Theatre and Theory.* Ed. Helene Keyssar. New York: St. Martin's, 1966. 19–34.

Fuchs, Elinor. "Adrienne Kennedy and the First Avant-Garde." *Intersecting Boundaries: The Theatre of Adrienne Kennedy.* Eds. Paul K. Bryant-Jackson and Lois More Overbeck. Minneapolis: U of Minnesota P, 1992. 76–84.

Geis, Deborah. "'A Spectator Watching My Life': Adrienne Kennedy's *A Movie Star Has to Star in Black and White.*" *Intersecting Boundaries: The Theatre of Adrienne Kennedy.* Eds. Paul K. Bryant-Jackson and Lois More Overbeck. Minneapolis: U of Minnesota P, 1992. 170–178.

Gillespie, Patti. "American Women Dramatists 1960-1980." *Essays on Contemporary American Drama.* Ed. Hedwig Bock and Albert Wertheim. Munich: M. Hueber, 1981. 187-206.

Grossman, Samuel L. "Trends in the Avant-Garde Theatre of the United States During the 1960's." Diss. Univ. of Minnesota, 1974.

"The Growth of Images." *The Drama Review* 21 (1977): 41–47.

Hatch, James. "Speak to Me in Those Old Words, You Know, Those La-La Words, Those Tung-Tung Sounds (Some African Influences on the Afro-American Theatre)." *Yale/Theatre* 8 (Fall 1976): 25-34.

Hay, Samuel A. "African-American Drama, 1950-1970." *Negro History Bulletin* 36 (1973): 5-8.

———. *African American Theatre: An Historical and Critical Analysis.* Cambridge: Cambridge Univ. Press, 1994.

Herman, William. "Playwrights at Work: Other Voices." *Understanding Contemporary Drama.* Columbia, SC: Univ. of South Carolina Press, 1987. 230-249.

Hooks, Bell. "Critical Reflections: Adrienne Kennedy, The Writer, The Work." *Intersecting Boundaries: The Theatre of Adrienne Kennedy.* Eds. Paul K. Bryant-Jackson and Lois More Overbeck. Minneapolis: U of Minnesota P, 1992. 179–185.

Jenkins, Linda W. "Locating the Language of Gender Experience." *Women & Performance* 2 (1984): 5-20.

"Kennedy, Adrienne." *Black Writers: A Selection of Sketches from Contemporary Authors.* Detroit: Gale, 1989.

Keyssar, Helen. "Rites and Responsibilites: The Drama of Black American Women." *Feminine Focus: The New Women Playwrights.* Ed. Enoch Brater. Cambridge: Oxford University Press, 1989. 226-240.

Kintz, Linda. "The Dramaturgy of the Subject(s): Refining the Deconstruction and Construction of the Subject to Include Gender and Materiality." *DAI* 47/07 (1986): 2574A. University of Oregon.

———. "The Sanitized Spectacle: What's Birth Got to Do With It? Adrienne Kennedy's *A Movie Star Has to Star in Black and White.*" *Theatre Journal* 44 (March 1992): 67-86.

Kolin, Philip C. "From the Zoo to the Funnyhouse: A Comparison of Edward Albee's *The Zoo Story* with Adrienne Kennedy's *Funnyhouse of a Negro.*" *Theatre-Southwest* Apr. 1989: 8-16.

————. "Color Connections in Adrienne Kennedy's *She Talks to Beethoven.*" *Notes on Contemporary Literature* 24 (March 1994): 4–6.

————. "Orpheus Ascending: Music, Race, and Gender in Adrienne Kennedy's *She Talks to Beethoven.*" *African-American Review* 28 (Summer 1994): 293-304.

Lewis, Allan. "Trends of the Decade." *American Plays and Playwrights of the Contemporary Theatre.* New York: Crown, 1965; rev. ed. 1970. 243- 257.

Magill, Frank N. "Adrienne Kennedy." *Great Women Writers: The Lives and Works of 135 of the World's Most Important Women Writers, From Antiquity to the Present.* New York: Holt and Co., 1994.

Mason, Louise. "The Fight to be an American Woman and a Playwright: A Critical History from 1773 to the Present." Diss. Univ. of California, Berkeley, 1983.

Meigs, Susan. "No Place but the Funnyhouse: The Struggle for Identity in Three Adrienne Kennedy Plays." *Modern American Drama.* Ed. June Schlueter. Rutherford, NJ: Fairleigh Dickinson Univ. Press, 1990. 172- 183.

Miller, Jeanne-Marie. "Black Women Playwrights from Grimké to Shange: Selected Synopses of Their Works." *But Some of Us Are Brave: Black Women's Studies.* Ed. Gloria Hull, P.B. Scott, and Barbara Smith. Old Westbury, NY: Feminist Press, 1982. 280–290.

————. "Images of Black Women in Plays by Black Playwrights." *CLA Journal* 20 (June 1977): 494-507. Rpt. as "Black Women in Plays by Black Playwrights." *Women in American Theatre.* Ed. Helen Krich Chinoy and Linda W. Jenkins. New York: Theatre Communications Group, 1987. 254- 259.

Mitchell, Loften. "The 1960s: Broadway Reconsidered." *Black Drama: The Story of the American Negro in Theatre.* New York: Hawthorne Books, 1967. 183-224.

Murray, Timothy. "Screening the Camera's Eye: Black and White Confrontations of Technical Representation." *Modern Drama* 28 (1985): 110-124.

Ogunbiyi, Yemi. "New Black Playwrights in America, 1960-1975." Diss. New York Univ., 1976.

Olauson, Judith. *The American Woman Playwright: A View of Criticism and Characterization*. Troy, NY: Whitson, 1981.

Overbeck, Lois More. "The Life of the Work: A Preliminary Sketch." *Intersecting Boundaries: The Theatre of Adrienne Kennedy*. Eds. Paul K. Bryant-Jackson and Lois More Overbeck. Minneapolis: U of Minnesota P, 1992. 21–41.

Patsalidis, Savas. "Adrienne Kennedy's Heterotopias and the (Im)Possibilities of the (Black) Female Self." *Stage Difference: Cultural Pluralism in American Theatre and Drama*. Ed. Marc Maufort. New York: Peter Lang, 1995. 301–321.

Peterson, Bernard L. "Kennedy, Adrienne." *Contemporary Black American Playwrights*. Westport, CT: Greenwood, 1988.

Rahman, Aishah. "To Be Black, Female, and a Playwright." *Freedomways* 19 (1979): 256-260.

Robinson, Alice, Vera Mowry Roberts, and Milly Barranger. "Adrienne Kennedy." *Notable Women in American Theatre: A Biographical Dictionary*. Westport, CT: Greenwood, 1989.

Scanlan, Robert. "Surrealism as Mimesis: A Director's Guide to Adrienne Kennedy's *Funnyhouse of a Negro*." *Intersecting Boundaries: The Theatre of Adrienne Kennedy*. Ed. Paul K. Bryant-Jackson and Lois More Overbeck. Minneapolis: U of Minnesota P, 1992. 93–109.

Shinn, Thelma. "Living the Answer: The Emergence of African-American Feminist Drama." *Studies in the Humanities* 17 (Dec. 1990): 149-159.

Simon, John. *Uneasy Stages: A Chronicle of the New York Theater, 1963-1973*. New York: Random House, 1975.

Sollors, Werner. "Owls and Rats in the American Funnyhouse: Adrienne Kennedy's Drama." *American Literature* 63 (Sept. 1991): 507-532.

———. "*People Who Led to My Plays*: Adrienne Kennedy's Autobiography." *Intersecting Boundaries: The Theatre of Adrienne Kennedy*. Eds. Paul K. Bryant-Jackson and Lois More Overbeck. Minneapolis: U of Minnesota P, 1992. 13–20.

Sontag, Susan. "Going to the Theater (and the Movies)." *Partisan Review* 31 (Spring 1964): 284-294.

Splawn, P. Jane. "Adrienne Kennedy." *Critical Survey of Drama: Supplement.* Ed. Frank Magill. Pasadena: Salem Press, 1987. 212-217.

Talbot, William. "Every Negro in His Place." *Drama Critique* 7 (Spring 1964): 92-95.

Terner, Robert L. "Theatre of Identity: Adrienne Kennedy's Portrait of the Black Woman." *Studies in Black Literature* 6 (1975): 1-5.

Thomas, Cathy. "The Daughter and Her Journey of Self-Definition in the Familial Plays of Adrienne Kennedy." A.B. honors thesis, Harvard Univ., 1985.

Turner, Beth. "Beyond Funnyhouse: Adrienne Kennedy." *Black Masks* 1 (Dec. 1984): 1, 8-9.

Turner, Darwin T. "Negro Playwrights and the Urban Negro." *CLA Journal* 12 (Sept. 1968): 19-25.

Turner, S.H. Regina. "Images of Black Women in the Plays of Black Female Playwrights, 1950-1975." *DAI* 43/01 (1982): 19A. Bowling Green State University.

Wilkerson, Margaret B. "Diverse Angles of Vision: Two Black Women Playwrights." *Theatre Annual* 40 (1985): 91-114.

———. "Adrienne Kennedy." *Dictionary of Literary Biography.* Vol. 38. Detroit: Gale Research, 1985.

Wilkerson, Margaret E. "Diverse Angles of Vision: Two Black Women Playwrights." *Intersecting Boundaries: The Theatre of Adrienne Kennedy.* Eds. Paul K. Bryant-Jackson and Lois More Overbeck. Minneapolis: U of Minnesota P, 1992. 58–75.

Williams, Mance. *Black Theatre in the 1960s and 1970s: A Historical-Critical Analysis of the Movement.* Westport, CT: Greenwood, 1985.

Zinman, Toby S. "'In the Presence of Mine Enemies': Adrienne Kennedy's *An Evening with Essex.*" *Studies in American Drama: 1945-Present* 6 (1991): 3-13.

C39. KIMBALL, KATHLEEN

C39.1. ———. *Meat Rack. Scripts #7* (New York Shakespeare Festival Public Theatre) May 1972: 81-85.

A one-act drama that examines the mentality of a black prostitute who wants to leave her profession.

Secondary Sources
Scholarly Criticism
Peterson, Bernard L. "Kimball, Kathleen." *Contemporary Black American Playwrights.* Westport, CT: Greenwood, 1988.

C40. LENOIRE, ROSETTA

C40.1. ———. *Bubbling Brown Sugar.* New York: Broadway Publishing Co., 1984.

The two-act musical revue reflects numerous all-black musical revues from 1910 to 1940. Featured music includes works by such artists as Duke Ellington, Billie Holiday, Cab Calloway, and J.C. Johnson.

Secondary Sources
General Articles
Carter, Patricia A. "*Essence* Woman." *Essence* May 1987: 30.

Scholarly Criticism
Norflett, Linda K. "The Theatre Career of Rosetta Lenoire." *DAI* 44/09 (1983): 2626A. New York Univ.

———. "Rosetta LeNoire: The Lady and Her Theatre." *Black American Literature Forum* 17 (Summer 1983): 69-72.

Peterson, Bernard L. "Lenoire, Rosetta." *Contemporary Black American Playwrights.* Westport, CT: Greenwood, 1988.

C41. LINCOLN, ABBEY

C41.1. ———. *A Streak o' Lean.* Excerpt in *Black Scenes.* Ed. Alice Childress. Garden City, NY: Zenith Books, 1971. 47-55.

A full-length drama that tests the moral decisions of a black man after he finds a substantial sum of money.

Secondary Sources
General Articles
DeVeaux, Alexis. "Do Be Do Wow!" *Essence* Oct. 1986: 54-65.

Scholarly Criticism
Bigelow Barbara C., ed. "Abbey Lincoln." *Contemporary Black Biography: Profiles From the International Black Community*. 6 Vols. Detroit: Gale Research, 1993.

Peterson, Bernard L. "Lincoln, Abbey." *Contemporary Black American Playwrights*. Westport, CT: Greenwood, 1988.

Smith, Jessie C., ed. "Abbey Lincoln." *Notable Black American Women*. Detroit: Gale Research, 1992.

C42.   MCCAULEY, ROBBIE

C42.1.   ———. *Sally's Rape*. *Moon Marked and Touched by Sun*. Ed. Sydné Mahone. New York: Theatre Communications Group, 1994. 218-238.

The one-act drama "reveal[s] the historical precedence for the use of rape as a tool of oppression" (Mahone xxix).

Primary Works About Drama
McCauley, Robbie. "Mississippi Freedom: North and South." *Theatre* 24 (1993): 88–98.

Secondary Sources
Scholarly Criticism
Murray, Timothy. "In Exile at Home: Tornado Breath and Unrighteous Fantasy in Robbie McCauley's Indian Blood." *Discourse: Journal for Theoretical Studies in Media and Culture* 16 (Spring 1994): 29–45.

Patraka, Vivian M. "Robbie McCauley: Obsessing in Public (Interview)." *The Drama Review* 37 (Summer 1993): 25-55.

Peterson, Bernard L. "Patraka, Vivian." *Contemporary Black American Playwrights*. Westport, CT: Greenwood, 1988.

Willinges, David. "Developing a Concert for the Spoken Voice: Solo Voyages and An Interview with Robbie McCauley." *Intersecting Boundaries: The Theatre of Adrienne Kennedy*. Eds. Paul K. Bryant-Jackson and Lois More Overbeck. Minneapolis: U of Minnesota P, 1992. 224–230.

C43.   MARTIN, SHARON STOCKARD

C43.1.   ———. *Proper and Fine: Fanny Lou Hamer's Entourage*. New York: Scholastic Book Services, 1972.

The one-act drama is, according to *CBAP*, "about two black shoppers, loaded down with goods, who wait to be waited on by an indifferent salesman in a department store in the segregated South" (331).

C43.2.   ———. *The Moving Violation*. *Center Stage*. Ed. Eileen Ostrow. Oakland: Sea Urchin Press, 1981. 125-153.

A two-act drama that examines the treatment of a family whose freedoms are systematically taken from them.

Secondary Sources
Scholarly Criticism
Peterson, Bernard L. "Martin, Sharon Stockard." *Contemporary Black American Playwrights*. Westport, CT: Greenwood, 1988.

C44.   MASON, JUDI ANN

C44.1.   ———. *Livin' Fat*. New York: Samuel French, 1976.

The two-act drama is centered around the family of a bank janitor who found $15,000 after a bank robbery. The family's dilemma is that they belong to a strict religious sect, and their newly found money threatens their high moral standards.

Secondary Sources
General Articles
Coleman, Wanda. "Black Writers in the Theater: A Gray Future?" *New York Times* 17 July 1977: 56.

Johnson, Pamela. "Judi Ann Mason." *Essence* Oct. 1987: 27.

Lesem, Jeanne. "Writer's Plays Show Life As It Really Is." *Chicago Defender* 20 Aug. 1977: 13. Rpt. in *Atlanta Daily World* 1 Sept. 1977: 7.

Stinson, Patricia. "*Essence* Women: Judi Ann Mason." *Essence* Nov. 1977: 6.

Scholarly Criticism
Peterson, Bernard L. "Mason, Judi Ann." *Contemporary Black American Playwrights*. Westport, CT: Greenwood, 1988.

Williams, Mance. *Black Theatre in the 1960s and 1970s: A Historical-Critical Analysis of the Movement*. Westport, CT: Greenwood, 1985.

C45.   NSABE, NIA

C45.1.   ————. *Moma Don't Know What Love Is. Three Hundred and Sixty Degrees of Blackness Comin' at You*. Ed. Sonia Sanchez. New York: 5X Publishing, 1971. n. pag.

The one-act drama explores the relationship between a mother and daughter after the daughter becomes pregnant at a young age just as her mother did. The mother's hope was that she could have protected her daughter from the painful experience.

Secondary Sources

Scholarly Criticism
Peterson, Bernard L. "nSabe, Nia." *Contemporary Black American Playwrights*. Westport, CT: Greenwood, 1988.

C46.   O'NEAL, REGINA

C46.1.   ————. *And Then the Harvest. And Then the Harvest: Three Television Plays*. Regina O'Neal. Detroit: Broadside Press, 1974. 69-103.

The one-act drama explores the race riots of the 1960s and the causes. It is centered around a black family that moves to a northern ghetto from the South.

C46.2.   ————. *Night Watch*. O'Neal 105-142.

The drama "explores the shallow nature of white liberalism when put to an actual test involving a black" (*CBAP* 362).

C46.3.   ————. *Walk a Tight Rope*. O'Neal 16-67.

The drama deals with the experiences of a young black teacher who is the first black assigned to teach at an all-white school during the 1960s.

Secondary Sources
Scholarly Criticism
Peterson, Bernard L. "O'Neal, Regina." *Contemporary Black American Playwrights*. Westport, CT: Greenwood, 1988.

C47.   **OSBORNE, PEGGY A.**

C47.1.   ———. *The Meeting*. Chicago: Afro-American Publishing Co., 1968.

A one-act educational play designed for classroom production by young students that highlights the achievements of such black personalities as Sidney Poitier, Jean Baptiste Point du Sable, and Frederick Douglass.

Secondary Sources
Scholarly Criticism
Peterson, Bernard L. "Osborne, Peggy." *Contemporary Black American Playwrights*. Westport, CT: Greenwood, 1988.

C48.   **PARKS, SUZAN-LORI**

C48.1.   ———. *The Death of the Last Black Man in the Whole Entire World. Moon Marked and Touched by Sun.* Ed. Sydné Mahone. New York: Theatre Communications Group, 1994. 249-279.

The full-length drama searches for the key to identity while revealing the tension of the human experience.

Secondary Sources
General Articles
Heilpem, John. "Voices From the Edge." *Vogue* Nov. 1993: 174+.

Scholarly Criticism
Rayner, Alice, and Harry J. Elam, Jr. "Unfinished Business: Reconfiguring History in Suzan-Lori Park's *The Death of the Last Black Man in the Whole Entire World*." *Theatre Journal* 46 (Dec. 1994): 447-461.

Robinson, Marc. "Four Writers." *Theater* 21 (Summer-Fall 1990): 73-80.

Solomon, Alisa. "Signifying on the Signifyin': The Plays of Suzan-Lori Parks." *Theater* 21 (Summer-Fall 1990): 73-80.

C49.   **RAHMAN, AISHAH**

C49.1.   ———. *Unfinished Women Cry in No Man's Land While a Bird Dies in a Gilded Cage. Nine Plays by Black Women.* Ed. Margaret Wilkerson. New York: Penguin Books, 1986. 199-237.

A twelve-scene drama that examines the needs and wants of teenage mothers.

C49.2.   ———. *Lady and the Tramp. Confirmation: An Anthology of African American Women.* Ed. Amiri and Amina Baraka. New York: William Morrow, 1983. 265-284.

The full-length drama, according to *CBAP*, "deals with the problem of male-female alienation in contemporary society" (390).

C49.3.   ———. *Transcendental Blues.* Baraka 284-299.

The full-length drama is a companion piece to *Lady and the Tramp* that is "about a middle-aged woman who is abandoned by her young lover" (*CBAP* 389).

C49.4.   ———. *The Mojo and the Sayso. Massachusetts Review* 39 (Spring 1988): 169-216. Rpt. in *Moon Marked and Touched by Sun.* Ed. Sydné Mahone. New York: Theatre Communications Group, 1994. 286-320.

The two-act drama, according to the author's notes, "is a story of a family: vulnerable human beings who sustain pain and love, hatreds, fears, joys, sorrows and degradation, and finally triumph" (Mahone 286).

Secondary Sources

General Articles
Gossett, Hattie. "Aishah Rahman: Transcending the Black Woman's Blues." *N. Y. Amsterdam News* 24 Sept. 1977, sec. D: 8.

Scholarly Criticism
Koger, Alicia K. "Jazz Form and Jazz Function: An Analysis of *Unfinished Women Cry in No Man's Land While a Bird Dies in a Gilded Cage.*" *Melus* 16 (Fall 1989-90): 99-111.

Peterson, Bernard L. "Rahman, Aishah." *Contemporary Black American Playwrights.* Westport, CT: Greenwood, 1988.

Rahman, Aishah. "To Be Black, Female, and a Playwright." *Freedomways* 19 (1979): 256-260.

"Tradition and a New Aesthetic." *Melus* 16 (Fall 1989-90): 23-26.

Wilkerson, Margaret. "Music as Metaphor: New Plays of Black Women." *Making a Spectacle: Feminist Essays on Contemporary Women's Theatre*. Ed. Lynda Hart. Ann Arbor: Univ. of Michigan Press, 1989. 61-75.

C50. REED, EDWINA

C50.1. ———. *A Man Always Keeps His Word. Negro History Bulletin* (Jan. 1963): 138-140.

The one-act drama reflects President Lincoln's decision to write the Emancipation Proclamation.

Secondary Sources
Scholarly Criticism
Peterson, Bernard L. "Reed, Edwina." *Contemporary Black American Playwrights*. Westport, CT: Greenwood, 1988.

C51. RHODES, CRYSTAL

C51.1. ———. *The Trip. Center Stage*. Ed. Eileen Ostrow. Oakland: Sea Urchin Press, 1981. 207-217.

The one-act drama explores the relationship of four women friends who take a trip from Chicago to California. As they ride in the car, they begin to irritate each other beyond belief, each one highlighting the flaws of the three others, until they can stand to be in each others' presence no longer.

Secondary Sources
Scholarly Criticism
Peterson, Bernard L. "Rhodes, Crystal." *Contemporary Black American Playwrights*. Westport, CT: Greenwood, 1988.

C52. RICHARDS, BEAH

C52.1. ———. *A Black Woman Speaks. Nine Plays by Black Women*. Ed. Margaret Wilkerson. New York: Penguin Books, 1986. 33-39.

A one-woman monologue that encourages white women to see themselves enslaved by male dominance to the same degree that Black women
were enslaved by whites.

Secondary Sources

General Articles
"Beah Richards." *Ebony* Oct. 1987: 61+.

Scholarly Criticism
Peterson, Bernard L. "Richards, Beah." *Contemporary Black American
Playwrights.* Westport, CT: Greenwood, 1988.

Smith, Jessie C., ed. "Beah Richards." *Notable Black American Women.*
Detroit: Gale Research, 1992.

C53.   **SANCHEZ, SONIA**

C53.1.   ————. *The Bronx Is Next. The Drama Review* 12 (Summer 1968):
78-83; Rpt. in *Cavalcade: Negro American Writing from 1760 to the
Present.* Ed. Arthur P. Davis and J. Saunders Redding. Boston: Houghton Miflin, 1971. 811-819.

The one-act drama attacks poor housing standards in the Bronx and in
Harlem.

C53.2.   ————. "Dirty Hearts." *Scripts #1* (New York Shakespeare Festival
Public Theatre) (Nov. 1971): 46-50.

A one-act drama that uses the game of Dirty Hearts as "a metaphor for
race relations in America; the game is conducted by white men, and the
black man always gets the Queen of Spades, which causes him to lose the
game" (*CBAP* 412).

C53.3.   ————. *Sister Son/ji. Wines in the Wilderness.* Ed. Elizabeth Brown-
Guillory. Westport, CT: Greenwood Press, 1990. 151-162; *New Plays
from the Black Theatre.* Ed. Ed Bullins. New York: Bantam Books,
1969. 97-107.

The one-act monologue examines the search of a black woman for her
identity. Her search parallels the struggle of blacks in America.

C53.4.   ————. *Uh, Uh: But How Do It Free Us? The New Lafayette Theatre
Presents.* Ed. Ed Bullins. Garden City, NY: Anchor Press, 1974. 165-
215.

The three-scene drama examines male/female relationships in the struggle for personal freedom.

C53.5.   ————. "Malcolm Man Don't Live Here No Mo!" *Black Theatre #6* (1972): n. pag.

The one-act children's play examines the ideals of Malcolm X.

Primary Works About Drama

Sanchez, Sonia. "Ruminations/Reflections." In *Black Women Writers*. Ed. Mari Evans. Garden City, NY: Anchor Press, 1984. 415-418.

Secondary Sources

General Articles

Cornwell, Anita. "Attuned to the Energy: Sonia Sanchez." *Essence* July 1979: 10.

Scholarly Criticism

Adams, Julyette Tamy. "Keepers of the Oral Traditions: An Afrocentric Analysis of Representative Plays by African-American Females, 1970–1984." *DAI* 57/01 (1995): 0210. Bowling Green State U.

Baker, Jr., Houston. "Our Lady: Sonia Sanchez and the Writing of a Black Renaissance." *Reading Black, Reading Feminist.* Eds. Joe Weixlmann and Houston A. Baker, Jr. Greenwood, FL: Penkevill, 1988. 169-202.

Basel, Marilyn K. "Sanchez, Sonia." *Black Writers: A Selection of Sketches from Contemporary Authors.* Detroit: Gale Research, 1989.

Brown-Guillory, Elizabeth. "Six Female Black Playwrights: Images of Blacks in Plays by Lorraine Hansberry, Alice Childress, Sonia Sanchez, Barbara Molette, Martie Charles, and Ntozake Shange." *DAI* 41/07 (1980): 3104A. Florida State Univ.

Case, Sue-Ellen. *Feminism and Theatre.* New York: Methuen, 1988.

Claiborne, Jon L. "Modern Black Drama and the Gay Image." *College English* 36 (1974): 381-384.

Clark, Sebastian. "Sonia Sanchez and Her Work." *Black World* 20 (1971): 44–48, 96–98.

Curb, Rosemary K. "Pre-Feminism in the Black Revolutionary Drama of Sonia Sanchez." *Many Forms of Drama*. Ed. Karelisa Hartigan. New York: Univ. Press of America, 1985. 19-29.

Fabre, Genevieve. *Drumbeats, Masks and Metaphors: Contemporary Afro-American Theatre*. Cambridge: Harvard University Press, 1983.

Kalamu ya Salaam. "Sonia Sanchez." *Dictionary of Literary Biography*. Vol. 11. Detroit: Gale Research, 1985.

Keyssar, Helen. "Rites and Responsibilities: The Drama of Black American Women." *Feminine Focus: The New Women Playwrights*. Ed. Enoch Brater. Cambridge: Oxford Univ. Press, 1989. 226-240.

Mabhubuti, Haki. "Sonia Sanchez: The Bringer of Memories." *Black Women Writers (1950–1980): A Critical Evaluation*. Ed. Mari Evans. Garden City, NY: Anchor-Doubleday, 1984. 419–432.

Melhem, D. H. "Sonia Sanchez: Will and Spirit." *Melus* 12 (Fall 1985): 73- 98.

Miller, Jeanne-Marie A. "Black Women Playwrights from Grimké to Shange: Selected Synopses of Their Works." *But Some of Us Are Brave: Black Women's Studies*. Ed. Gloria Hull, P.B. Scott, and Barbara Smith. Old Westbury, NY: Feminist Press, 1982. 280-290.

———. "Sanchez, Sonia." *Dictionary of the Black Theatre*. Westport, CT: Greenwood, 1983. 246-248.

Peterson, Bernard L. "Sanchez, Sonia." *Contemporary Black American Playwrights*. Westport, CT: Greenwood, 1988.

Rahman, Aishah. "To Be Black, Female, and a Playwright." *Freedomways* 19 (1979): 256-260.

Smith, Jessie C., ed. "Sonia Sanchez." *Notable Black American Women*. Detroit: Gale Research, 1992.

"Sonia Sanchez." *Black American Women Poets and Dramatists*. Ed. Harold Bloom. New York: Chelsea House, 1996. 189–203.

Tate, Claudia. "Sonia Sanchez." *Black Women Writers at Work*. New York: Continuum, 1983.

Taylor, Willene P. "The Reversal of the Tainted Blood Theme in the Works of Writers of the Black Revolutionary Theater." *Negro American Literature Forum* 10 (Fall 1976): 89-94.

Turner, S.H. Regina. "Images of Black Women in the Plays of Black Female Playwrights, 1950-1975." *DAI* 43/01 (1982): 19A. Bowling Green State Univ.

Walker, Barbara. "Sonia Sanchez Creates Poetry for the Stage." *Black Creation* 5 (Fall 1973): 12-14.

Williams, Mance. *Black Theatre in the 1960s and 1970s: A Historical-Critical Analysis of the Movement.* Westport, CT: Greenwood, 1985.

C54.   SHANGE, NTOZAKE

C54.1.   ———. *for colored girls who have considered suicide/when the rainbow is enuf.* New York: Macmillan, 1977; Rpt. London: Eyre Methuen, 1978; New York: Banton Books, 1980; Samuel French, 1981. Rpt. in *Totem Voices: Plays from the Black World Repertory.* Ed. Paul C. Harrison. New York: Grove Press, 1989. 223-274; *Plays, One.* Ntozake Shange. London: Methuen Drama, 1992. 1-66; *Best American Plays: Eighth Series 1974-1982.* Ed. Clive Barnes. New York: Crown, 1983. 82-105.

The full-length choreopoem explores the wants and desires of black women while exposing men as the source of their weaknesses.

C54.2.   ———. *A Photograph: Lovers-in-Motion.* New York: Samuel French, 1977. Rpt. in *Three Pieces.* Ntozake Shange. New York: St. Martin's Press, 1981/ Penguin Books, 1992. 53-108.

The two-act play examines the life of a misogynistic photographer and the three women in his life. The photographer's life takes a turn for the worse when he fails to win a fellowship that he deems necessary to establish his career.

C54.3.   ———. *Boogie Woogie Landscapes.* Shange. *Three Pieces,* 109-142.

A full-length theatre piece that presents a woman's experiences and dreams through song and dance. Shange uses the stream-of-consciousness technique to examine what it means to be a black woman in America.

C54.4.   ———. *spell #7: geechee jibara quik magic trance manual for technologically stressed third world people: A Theater Piece.* New York:
Samuel French, 1981; Rpt. London: Methuen, 1985. Rpt. in *Nine Plays
by Black Women.* Ed. Margaret Wilkerson. New York: Penguin Books,
1986. 243-291; Shange. *Three Pieces,* 1-52; Shange. *Plays, One,* 71-118.

A two-act choreopoem that examines how society dictates the social,
political, and personal roles of black men and women.

C54.5.   ———. *A Daughter's Geography.* New York: St. Martin's Press, 1983.
Rpt. as *Bocas: A Daughter's Geography.* New York: Samuel French,
1983.

The full-length choreopoem explores the topology of women. It also
examines the lives of Black people in America from slavery to recent
years as seen by the Cosmic Couple, Conarky and Tulsa.

C54.6.   ———. *From Okra to Greens: A Different Love Story.* New York:
Samuel French, 1983; St. Louis: Coffee House, 1984.

A full-length drama that highlights the differences in male and female
perspectives on love. In attempting to explain these differences, the
characters notice how many similarities emerge.

C54.7.   ———. *Daddy Says. New Plays for the Black Theatre.* Ed. Woodie
King, Jr. Chicago: Third World Press, 1989. 233-252.

The one-act drama examines the attempt of a father to raise his two
daughters after the death of his wife and their mother.

C54.8.   ———. *I Heard Eric Dolphy in His Eyes.* Shange. *Plays, One,* 159-178.

A full-length performance piece that explores "the violence and lyricism,
the incongruities and the constants, as well as the magic and limitations
of Afro- American urban life" (Shange. *Plays, One,* 160).

C54.9.   ———. *The Love Space Demands.* Shange. *Plays, One,* 131-158.

A series of theatre pieces that focus on issues ranging from sexuality to
feminism, each questioning the status quo.

C54.10.   ———. (With Emily Mann) *Betsy Brown: A Rhythm Blues Musical.*
Excerpt in *Studies in American Drama, 1945-Present* 4 (1989): 3-20.

The full-length dramatic musical satirizes a young girl's lesson on becoming a woman.

C54.11. ———. *The Resurrection of the Daughter: Liliane*. Excerpt in *Moon Marked and Touched by Sun*. Ed. Sydné Mahone. New York: Theatre Communications Group, 1994. 329-352.

The full-length theatre piece which was adapted from Shange's novel of the same title "chronicles the journey of a visual artist from adolescence to womanhood" (Mahone 327).

Primary Works About Drama

———. Introduction. *for colored girls who have considered suicide/ when the rainbow is enuf: a choreopoem*. By Shange. New York: Macmillan Publishing Co., 1977. ix-xvi.

———. "Ntozake Shange Interviews Herself." *Ms*. Dec. 1977: 35, 70-72.

———. "uncovered losses/black theater traditions." *Black Scholar* 10 (July/Aug. 1979): 7-9. Rpt. in *See No Evil: Prefaces, Essays & Accounts 1976-1983*. Ntozake Shange. San Francisco: Momo's Press, 1983. 4-6.

———. *See No Evil: Prefaces, Essays & Accounts 1976-1983*. San Francisco: Momo's Press, 1983.

Secondary Sources

General Articles

Allen, Bonnie. "A Home Instinct." *Essence* Aug. 1980: 17, 20.

Arkatov, Janice. "A Less-Public Obie Winner Writes On." *Los Angeles Times* 28 July 1987, sec. 6: 5.

Buckley, Tom. "The Three Stages of Ntozake Shange." *New York Times* 16 Dec. 1977: C6.

Considine, Shaun. "On Stage: Ntozake Shange." *People Weekly* 5 July 1976: 68-69.

Dong, Stella. "Ntozake Shange." *Publisher's Weekly* 3 May 1985: 74-75.

Eder, Richard. "Stage: 'spell #7' by Ntozake Shange." *New York Times* 16 July 1979: 12.

Frazer, C. Gerald. "Theatre Finds an Incisive New Playwright." *New York Times* 16 June 1976: 53.

Funke, Phyllis. "Beneath the Surface of Shange." *Los Angeles Times* 7 Aug. 1977, Calendar sec. 54.

Futterman, Ellen. "Ntozake Shange Casts Her Eye on Texas." *St. Louis Post Dispatch* 15 Apr. 1987, sec. F: 1, 4.

Gillespie, Marcia A. "Ntozake Shange Talks with Marcia A. Gillespie." *Essence* May 1985: 122-124, 203-208.

Gussow, Mel. "Stage: 'Colored Girl' Evolves." *New York Times* 16 Sept. 1976: 53.

————. "Women Write New Chapter." *New York Times* 8 June 1979: C3.

————. "Stage: 'Mother Courage.'" *New York Times* 14 May 1980: 20.

————. "Women Playwrights Show New Strength." *New York Times* 15 Feb. 1981, sec. 2: 4, 24.

————. "Women Playwrights: New Voices in the Theater." *New York Times Magazine* 1 May 1983: 22-27.

Guthmann, Edward. "Shange's Fond Memories." *San Francisco Chronicle* 19 June 1987: 87.

"Interview: Ntozake Shange." *The New Yorker* 2 Aug. 1976: 17-19.

Johnston, Laurie. "*Colored Girls* Goes to Rikers Island and Hits Home." *New York Times* 14 Jan. 1977, sec. B: 2.

Latour, Martine. "Ntozake Shange: Driven Poet/Playwright." *Mademoiselle* 82 Sept. 1976: 182, 226.

Lauerman, Connie. "Stage to Novel: Broadway Wasn't 'Enuf' for Author." *Chicago Tribune* 21 Oct. 1982, sec. 4: 1, 6.

Lewis, Barbara. "*For colored girls who have considered suicide.*" *Essence* Nov. 1976: 119-120.

"Ntozake Shange." *New Yorker* 2 August 1976: 17-19.

Rogers, Curtis E. "Good Theatre But Poor Sociological Statement." *N. Y. Amsterdam News* 9 Oct. 1976: 3 8.

"Showstoppers." *Essence* Oct. 1982: 75-77.

Umrani, Munir. "Ntozake Shange: Woman Behind Colored Girls." *Bilalian News* 6 Jan. 1978: 28.

"Welcome to the Great Black Way!" *Time* 1 Nov. 1976: 72-76.

Wykoff, Peter C. "Ntozake Shange." *Houston Post* 26 May 1985, sec. F: 11.

Scholarly Criticism
Adams, Julyette Tamy. "Keepers of the Oral Traditions: An Afrocentric Analysis of Representative Plays by African-American Females, 1970–1984." *DAI* 57/01 (1995): 0210. Bowling Green State U.

Alexander, Elizabeth. "Collage: An Approach to Reading African-American Women's Literature." *DAI* 53/11 (1993): 3905A. U of Pennsylvania.

Anderlini, Serena W. "Gender and Desire in Contemporary Drama: Lillian Hellman, Natalia Ginzburg, Franca Rame, and Ntozake Shange." *DAI* 49/4 (1988): 809A. Univ. of California, Riverside.

————. "Drama or Performance Art? An Interview with Ntozake Shange." *Journal of Dramatic Theory and Criticism* 6 (Fall 1991): 85-97.

Betsko, Kathleen, and Rachel Koenig. "Ntozake Shange." *Interviews with Contemporary Women Playwrights*. New York: Beach Tree Books, 1987. 365-376.

Biggs, Melissa, ed. "Murdering the King's English." *In the Vernacular: Interviews at Yale with Sculptors of Culture*. New York : McFarland & Co., 1991. 68-71.

"The Black Scholar Reader's Forum on Black Male-Female Relations." *Black Scholar* 10 (May-June, 1979): 15-67.

Blackwell, Henry. "An Interview with Ntozake Shange." *Black American Literature Forum* 13 (Winter 1979): 134-138.

Brown, Janet. *"for colored girls who considered suicide."* Feminist
Drama: Definiton and Critical Analysis. Metuchen, NJ: Scarecrow
Press, 1979. 114- 132.

Brown-Guillory, Elizabeth. "Six Female Black Playwrights: Images of
Blacks in Plays by Lorraine Hansberry, Alice Childress, Sonia Sanchez,
Barbara Molette, Martie Charles, and Ntozake Shange." *DAI* 41/07
(1980): 3104A. Florida State Univ.

————. "Ntozake Shange." *Dictionary of Literary Biography*. Vol. 38.
Detroit: Gale Research, 1985.

————. "Contemporary Black Women Playwrights: A View From the
Other Half." *Helicon Nine* 14/15 (Summer 1986): 120-127.

————. "Black Women Playwrights: Exorcising Myths." *Phylon* 68
(Fall 1987): 230-238.

————. *Their Place on the Stage: Black Women Playwrights in
America*. Westport, CT: Greenwood, 1988.

Case, Sue-Ellen. *Feminism and Theatre*. New York: Methuen, 1988.

Christ, Carol P. "'i found god in myself . . . & loved her fiercely':
Ntozake Shange." *Diving Deep and Surfacing: Women Writers on
Spiritual Quest*. Boston: Beacon Press, 1980. 97-117.

Coven, Brenda. "Ntozake Shange." *American Women Dramatists of the
Twentieth Century: A Bibliography*. Metuchen, NJ: Scarecrow, 1982.

Cronacher, Karen. "Unmasking the Minstrel Mask's Black Magic in
Ntozake Shange's *spell #7*." *Theatre Journal* 44 (May 1992): 177-193.
Rpt. in *Feminist Theatre and Theory*. Ed. Helen Keyssar. New York: St.
Martin's, 1996. 189–212.

Curb, Rosemary K. "Re/cognition, Re/presentation, Re/creation in
Woman-Conscious Drama: The Seer, The Seen, The Scene, The Obscene." *Theater Journal* 37 (Oct. 1985): 302-316.

DeShazer, Mary K. "Rejecting Necrophilia: Ntozake Shange and the
Warrior Re-visioned." *Making a Spectacle: Feminist Essays on Contemporary Women's Theatre*. Ed. Lynda Hart. Ann Arbor: Univ. of Michigan Press, 1989. 86-100.

Dodson, Owen. "Who Has Seen the Wind? Playwrights and the Black Experience." *Black American Literature Forum* 11 (Fall 1977):108-116.

Early, James. "Interview with Ntozake Shange." *In Memory and Spirit of Frances, Zora, and Lorraine: Essays And Interviews on Black Women and Writing*. Ed. Juliette Bowles. Washington, DC: Institute for the Arts and the Humanities, Howard University, 1979. 23-26.

Effiong, Philip Uko. "The Subliminal to the Real: Musical Regeneration in Ntozake Shange's Boogie Woogie Landscapes." *Theatre Studies* 39 (1994): 33-43.

————. "In Search of a Model for African American Drama: The Example of Lorraine Hansberry, Amiri Baraka, and Ntozake Shange." *DAI* 55/07 (1995): 1744A. U of Wisconsin, Madison.

Elliot, Jeffrey. "Ntozake Shange: Genesis of a Choreopoem." *Negro History Bulletin* 41 (Jan.-Feb. 1978): 797-800.

Fabre, Genevieve. *Drumbeats, Masks and Metaphors: Contemporary Afro-American Theatre*. Cambridge: Harvard University Press, 1983.

Flowers, Sandra H. "Colored Girls: Textbook for the Eighties." *Black American Forum* 15 (Summer 1981): 51-54.

Foster, Karen K. "De-Tangling the Web: Mother-Daughter Relationships in the Plays of Marsha Norman, Lillian Helman, Tina Howe, and Ntozake Shange." *DAI* 55/10 (1995): 3041A. U of Nebraska, Lincoln.

Geis, Deborah. "Distraught Laughter: Monologue in Ntozake Shange's Theatre Pieces." *Feminine Focus: The New Women Playwrights*. Ed. Enoch Brater. New York: Oxford Univ. Press, 1989. 210-225.

Gillespie, Patti. "American Women Dramatists, 1960-1980." *Essays on Contemporary American Drama*. Eds. Hedwig Bock and Albert Wertheim. Munich: M. Hueber, 1981. 187-206.

Griffn, Gabriele. "'Writing the Body': Reading Joan Riley, Grace Nichols, and Ntozake Shange." *Black Women's Writing*. Ed. Gina Wisker. New York: St. Martin's Press, 1993. 19-42.

Hay, Samuel. *African American Theatre: An Historical and Critical Analysis*. Cambridge: Cambridge Univ. Press, 1994.

Hayes, Donald. "An Analysis of Dramatic Themes Used by Selected Black- American Playwrights from 1950-1976 with a Backgrounder: The State of the Art of Contemporary Black Theater and Black Play-wrighting." Diss. Wayne State Univ., 1984.

Jay, Julia De Foor. "Women's Identity Formations and the Intersecting Concepts of Gender, Race, and Class in the Plays of Ntozake Shange, Beth Henley, and Cherie Moraga." *DAI* 56/02 (1995): 407A. U of Houston.

Jordan, June. "Shange Talks the Real Stuff" *The Dial* Feb. 1982: 11-13.

Kent, Assunta. "The Rich Multiplicity of *Betsy Brown.*" *Journal of Dramatic Theory and Criticism* 7 (Fall 1992): 151–161.

Keyssar, Helen. "Rites and Responsibilities: The Drama of Black American Women." *Feminine Focus: The New Women Playwrights.* Ed. Enoch Brater. Cambridge: Oxford Univ. Press, 1989. 226-240.

Kim, Jeongho. "Shange's Writing: Discourse of the 'Other'." *The Journal of English Language and Literature* 40 (1994): 99-118.

———. "Discursive Strategy of Feminism Drama: Caryl Churchill and Ntozake Shange." *The Journal of English Language and Literature* 41 (1995): 533–555.

King, Anne Mills. "Ntozake Shange." *Critical Survey of Drama: Supplement.* Ed. Frank Magill. Pasadena: Salem Press, 1986. 326-331.

King, Jr., Woodie. *Black Theatre: Present Condition.* New York: Publishing Center for Cultural Resources, 1981.

Kolin, Philip, ed. "Ntozake Shange." *American Playwrights Since 1945.* New York: Greenwood, 1989.

LeSeur, Geta. "From Nice Colored Girl to Womanist: An Exploration of Development in Ntozake Shange's Writings." *Language and Literature in the African-American Imagination.* Ed. Carol A. Black-shire-Belay. Westport, CT: Greenwood, 1992. 167-180.

———. "An Interview with Ntozake Shange." *Studies in American Drama: 1945-Present* 5 (1990): 42-66.

———. "Shange's Men: *for colored girls* Revisited, and Movement Beyond." *African-American Review* 26 (Summer 1992): 319-328.

Lester, Neal A. "Ntozake Shange's Development of the Choreopoem."
DAI 49/05 (1988): 1142A. Vanderbilt Univ.

————. "An Interview with Ntozake Shange." *Studies in American
Drama* 5 (1990): 42–66.

————. "Shange's Men: *for colored girls* Revisited, and Movement
Beyond." *African American Review* 26 (Summer 1992): 319–328.

————. *Ntozake Shange: A Critical Study of the Plays.* New York:
Garland, 1995.

————. "Ntozake Shange." *Speaking on Stage: Interviews with Contemporary American Playwrights.* Eds. Philip C. Kolin and Colby H.
Kullman. Tuscaloosa: U of Alabama P, 1996. 216–229.

Levin, Tobe, and Gwendolyn Flowers. "Black Feminism in *for colored
girls.*" *History and Tradition in Afro-American Culture.* Ed. Gunter
Lenz. Frankfurt: Campus Verlag, 1984. 181-193.

Levine, Jo Ann. "'Bein' a Woman, Bein' Colored.'" *Christian Science
Monitor* 9 Sept. 1976: 23.

Lyons, Brenda. "Interview with Ntozake Shange." *Massachusetts
Review* 28 (Winter 1987): 687-697.

Mael, Phyllis. "Rainbow of Voices." *Women in American Theatre.* Ed.
Helen Chinoy and Linda W. Jenkins. New York: Theatre Communications Group, 1987. 317-321.

Magill, Frank N. "Ntozake Shange." *Great Women Writers: The Lives
and Works of 135 of the World's Most Important Women Writers, From
Antiquity to the Present.* New York: Holt and Co., 1994.

Mason, Louise C. "The Fight to be an American Woman and a
Playwright: A Critical History from 1773 to the Present." Diss. Univ. of
California, Berkley, 1983.

Miller, Jeanne-Marie A. "Black Women Playwrights from Grimké to
Shange: Selected Synopses of Their Works." *But Some of Us Are Brave:
Black Women's Studies.* Ed. Gloria Hull, P.B. Scott, and Barbara Smith.
Old Westbury, NY: Feminist Press, 1982. 280-290.

————. "Three Theatre Pieces by Ntozake Shange." *Theatre News* 14
(Apr. 1982): 8.

————. "Shange, Ntozake." *Dictionary of Black Theatre*. Westport, CT: Greenwood, 1983. 248-250.

Mitchell, Carolyn. "'A Laying On of Hands': Transcending the City in Ntozake Shange's *for colored girls*." *Women Writers and the City: Essays in Feminist Literary Criticism*. Ed. Susan M. Squier. Knoxville: Univ. of Tennessee Press, 1984. 230-248.

Murray, Timothy. "Screening the Camera's Eye: Black and White Confrontations of Technological Reproduction." *Modern Drama* 28 (Mar. 1985): 110-124.

Neal, Lester A. "At the Heart of Shange's Feminism: An Interview." *Black American Literature Forum* 24 (Winter 1990): 717-730.

"Ntozake Shange." *Black American Women Poets and Dramatists*. Ed. Harold Bloom. New York: Chelsea House, 1996. 204–218.

O'Connor, Mary. "Subject, Voice, and Women in Some Contemporary Black American Women's Writing." *Feminism, Bakhtin, and the Dialogic*. Eds. Dale M. Bauer and Susan Jaret McKinstry. Albany: State U of New York P, 1991. 199–217.

O'Rourke, Joyce W. "New Female Playwrights in the American Theatre, 1973-1983: A Critical Analysis of Thought in Selected Plays." Diss. Louisiana State Univ., 1988.

Olaniyan, Tejumola. "The Poetics and Politics of 'Othering': Contemporary African, African-American, and Caribbean Drama and the Invention of Cultural Identities." *DAI* 52/08 (1992): 2922A. Cornell U.

Patraka, Vivian. "Staging Memory: Contemporary Plays by Women." *Michigan Quarterly Review* 26 (Winter 1987): 285-292.

Peters, Erskine. "Some Tragic Propensities of Ourselves: The Occasion of Ntozake Shange's *for colored girls*." *Journal of Ethnic Studies* 6 (Spring 1978): 79-85.

Peterson, Bernard L. "Shange, Ntozake." *Contemporary Black American Playwrights*. Westport, CT: Greenwood, 1988.

Pinkney, Mikell. "Theatrical Expressionism in the Structure and Language of Ntozake Shange's *spell #7*." *Theatre Studies* 37 (1992): 5-15.

Qureshi, Amber. "Where the Womanisms Grow: Ritual and Romanticism in *for colored girls who have considered suicide.*" *Notes on Contemporary Literature* 26 (Sept. 1996): 6–8.

Ribowsky, Mark. "A Poetess Scores a Hit With Play On 'What's Wrong With Black Men'." *Sepia* 25 (Dec. 1976): 24-25.

Richards, Sandra L. "Conflicting Impulses in the Plays of Ntozake Shange." *Black American Literature Forum* 17 (Summer 1983): 73-78.

Roberts, Vera M. "Bright Lights and Backstage: Women Playwrights in the Theatre." *Furman Studies* 34 (Dec. 1988): 26-35.

Robinson, Alice M., Vera M. Roberts, and Milly Barranger. "Ntozake Shange." *Notable Women in the American Theatre: A Biographical Dictionary.* New York: Greenwood, 1989.

Rushing, Andrea B. *"for colored girls,* Suicide or Struggle." *Massachusetts Review* 22 (Autumn 1981): 539-550.

"Shange, Ntozake." *Black Writers: A Selection of Sketches from Contemporary Authors.* Detroit: Gale Research, 1989.

"Shange, Ntozake." *Major Twentieth Century Writers: A Selection of Sketches from Contemporary Authors.* Detroit: Gale Research, 1991.

Shinn, Thelma. "Living the Answer: The Emergence of African-American Feminist Drama." *Studies in the Humanities* 17 (Dec. 1990): 149-159.

Smith, Jessie C. "Ntozake Shange." *Epic Lives: One Hundred Black Women Who Made a Difference.* Detroit: Visible Ink Press, 1993.

Smith, Valerie, Lea Baechler, and A. Walton, eds. "Ntozake Shange." *African American Writers.* New York: Collier Books, 1993.

Splawn, P. Jane. "Rites of Passage in the Writing of Ntozake Shange: The Poetry, Drama, and Novels." *DAI* 50/3 (1989): 687A.

Staples, Robert. "The Myth of Black Macho: A Response To Angry Black Feminists." *Black Scholar* 10 (Mar./Apr. 1979): 24-32.

Talbert, Linda Lee. "Ntozake Shange: Scarlet Woman and Witch/Poet." *Umoja* 4 (Spring 1980): 5-10.

Tate, Claudia. "Ntozake Shange." *Black Women Writers at Work*. New York: Continuum, 1983. 149-174.

Thompson-Cager, Chezia. "Superstition, Magic and the Occult in Two Versions of Ntozake Shange's Choreopoem *for colored girls* and Novel *Sassafras, Cypress, and Indigo*." *MAWA Review* 4 (Dec. 1989): 37-41.

Timpane, John. "'The Poetry of the Moment': Politics and the Open Form in the Drama of Ntozake Shange." *Modern American Drama*. Ed. June Schlueter. Rutherford, NJ: Fairleigh Dickinson Univ. Press, 1990. 198-206. Rpt. in *Studies in American Drama* 4 (1989): 91–101.

Washington, Mary Helen. "Ntozake Shange." *The Playwright's Art: Conversations with Contemporary American Dramatists*. Ed. Jackson R. Bryer. New Brunswick, NJ: Rutgers UP, 1995. 205–220.

Waxman, Barbara F. "Dancing Out of Form, Dancing Into Self: Genre and Metaphor in Marshall, Shange, and Walker." *Melus* 19 (Fall 1994): 91-106.

Wilkerson, Margaret B. "Music as Metaphor: New Plays of Black Women." *Making a Spectacle: Feminist Essays on Contemporary Women's Theatre*. Ed. Lynda Hart. Ann Arbor: Univ. of Michigan Press, 1989. 61-75.

Williams, Mance. *Black Theatre in the 1960s and 1970s: A Historical-Critical Analysis of the Movement*. Westport, CT: Greenwood, 1985.

"Women and the Creative Process: A Discussion (with Susan Griffin, Norma Leistiko, Ntozake Shange, and Miriam Schapiro)." *Mosiac* 8 (1974-1975): 91-117.

C55.   **SMITH, ANNA DEAVERE**

C55.1.   ———. *Fires in the Mirror: Crown Heights, Brooklyn, and Other Identities*. New York: Anchor Books, 1993. Excerpt rpt. in *Moon Marked and Touched by Sun*. Ed. Sydné Mahone. New York: Theatre Communications Group, 1994. 361-380.

A series of theatre pieces that focus "on a timely event that has sparked controversy within the community" (Mahone xxx).

C55.2.   ———. *Twighlight: Los Angeles, 1992: On the Road, A Search For American Character*. New York: Anchor Books, 1994.

The full-length theatre piece reflects the thoughts, memories, and experiences of those directly affected by the riots in Los Angeles in 1992.

Secondary Sources

General Articles
Brock, Pope. "Anna Deavere Smith." *People Weekly* 30 Aug. 1993: 95+.

Chambers, Veronica. "Anna Deavere Smith: Acting Out the Madness." *Essence* Nov. 1993: 60.

Johnson, Pamela. Anna Deavere Smith: She is Bridging Our Vast Racial Divides through Theater." *Essence* Aug. 1994: 40+.

Rugoff, Ralph. "One Woman Chorus." *Vogue* April 1993: 224+.

Simon, Dawne E. "29 Characters in Search of Community." *Ms.* Sept./Oct. 1992: 67.

Scholarly Criticism
Bigelow, Barbara C., ed. "Anna Deavere Smith." *Contemporary Black Biography: Profiles from the International Black Community.* 6 vols. Detroit: Gale Research, 1994.

Lewis, Barbara L. "The Circle of Confusion: A Conversation with Anna Deavere Smith." *The Kenyon Review* 15 (Fall 1993): 54-64.

Lyons, Charles R., and James C. Lyons. "Anna Deavere Smith: Perspectives on her Performance within the Context of Critical Theory." *Journal of Dramatic Theory and Criticism* 9 (Fall 1994): 43-66.

Martin, Carol. "Anna Deavere Smith: The Word Becomes You—An Interview." *The Drama Review* 37 (Winter 1993): 45-62.

O'Rourke, Joyce W. "New Female Playwrights in the American Theatre, 1973-1983: A Critical Analysis of Thought in Selected Plays." Diss. Louisiana State University, 1988.

Rayner, Alice. "Improper Conjunctions: Metaphor, Performance, and Text." *Essays in Theatre* 14 (Nov. 1995): 3–14.

Rayner, Richard. "Word of Mouth." *Harper's Bazaar* April 1993: 248+.

Reinelt, Janelle. "Performing Race: Anna Devere Smith's *Fires in the Mirror.*" *Modern Drama* 39 (Winter 1996): 609–617.

Schechner, Richard. "Anna Deavere Smith: Acting as Incorporation." *The Drama Review* 37 (Winter 1993): 63-64.

Smith, Iris. "Authors in America: Tony Kushner, Arthur Miller, and Anna Deavere Smith." *The Centennial Review* 40 (Winter 1996): 125–142.

Sun, William H., and Faye C. Fei. "Masks or Faces Re-Visited: A Study of Four Theatrical Works Concerning Cultural Identity." *The Drama Review* 38 (1994): 120-132.

C56.   SMITH, JEAN WHEELER

C56.1.   ———. "O.C.'s Heart." *Negro Digest* (April 1970): 56-76.

The three-act drama is about a young man who retrieves his dead brother's heart after it had been given to a white man during a heart transplant.

Secondary Sources

Scholarly Criticism
Peterson, Bernard L. "Smith, Jean Wheeler." *Contemporary Black American Playwrights*. Westport, CT: Greenwood, 1988.

C57.   STILES, THELMA JACKSON

C57.1.   ———. *No One Man Show*. *Center Stage*. Ed. Eileen Ostrow. Oakland: Sea Urchin Press, 1981. 243-260.

The one-act drama examines the lives of two sisters and a brother after the death of their parents. The older sister, who is in her late thirties, takes responsibility for her siblings who are old enough to take care of themselves. When she realizes that she has allowed them to become too dependent upon her, she tries to make them both more independent.

Secondary Sources

Scholarly Criticism
Peterson, Bernard L. "Stiles, Thelma Jackson." *Contemporary Black American Playwrights*. Westport, CT: Greenwood, 1988.

C58. TAYLOR, REGINA

C58.1. ———. "Mudtracks." *Ensemble Studio Theatre (EST) Marathon 1994: One Act Plays.* Ed. Marissa Smith. Lyme, NH: Smith & Kraus, 1995. 202-224.

The twelve-scene drama examines the failed relationships of two generations of battered women.

Secondary Sources
General Articles
Allis, Tim. "A Matter of Character." *People Weekly* 23 March 1992: 75-76.

C59. TURNER, BETH

C59.1. ———. "Crisis at Little Rock." *Search* (A *Scholastic* magazine) 7 Apr. 1977: n. pag.

The one-act drama is about the historic desegregation of Central High School in Little Rock, Arkansas.

Secondary Sources
Scholarly Criticism
Peterson, Bernard L. "Turner, Beth." *Contemporary Black American Playwrights.* Westport, CT: Greenwood, 1988.

C60. VANCE, DANITRA

C60.1. ———. *Live and in Color! Moon Marked and Touched by Sun.* Ed. Sydné Mahone. New York: Theatre Communications Group, 1994. 389-406.

The two-part drama creates a "menagerie of zany characters [that] forms a lens through which we can scrutinize societal illness and recognize the ridiculous and ennobling ways in which we attempt to heal ourselves" (Mahone xxx).

Secondary Sources
General Articles
"Eye on . . . Scene-Stealers." *Harper's Bazaar* 120 (Aug. 1987): 158-161.

Hamilton, Stephanie R. "Showstopper." *Essence* Dec. 1984: 43.

Mason, Deborah. "That Black Girl." *Vogue* June 1986: 64.

C61.   **WALKER, LUCY M.**

C61.1.   ———. *A Dollar a Day Keeps the Doctor Away. Social Action in One-Act Plays*. Lucy Walker. Denver: Privately printed, 1970. n. pag.

The one-act drama "explores the inadequacy and inefficiency of neighborhood community health services, through the experiences of two patients in a doctor's office who are being treated very casually by a routine-oriented nurse" (*CBAP* 472).

C61.2.   ———. *Grades—Plus or Minus*. Walker n. pag.

The one-act drama is a debate about the symbolism and significance of grades after a young son is denied use of the family car until he improves his grades.

C61.3.   ———. *It's Only Money*. Walker n. pag.

The one-act drama reflects the experience of a couple whose furniture was repossessed because they failed to read the fine print before signing the contract.

C61.4.   ———. *My Own Man*. Walker n. pag.

The one-act drama examines the beginning of a political life of a young man who has just reached voting age. After listening to the rhetoric of candidates from both parties, the young man is still unable to decide which party to join.

C61.5.   ———. *The Real Estate Man*. Walker n. pag.

The one-act drama shows how a real estate agent will do anything to boost his sales including taking advantage of an unsuspecting couple. They sign the contract and soon after learn that, unfortunately, they knew too little about leases.

C61.6.   ———. *To Cuss or Bus*. Walker n. pag.

The one-act drama explores the advantages and disadvantages of school busing.

C61.7. ———. *We All Pay.* Walker n. pag.

The one-act drama examines the mistake of a mother in not coming to the aid of a screaming woman who is being raped because the mother does not want to get involved. She later learns that the screaming woman was her daughter.

Secondary Sources
Scholarly Criticism
Peterson, Bernard L. "Walker, Lucy M." *Contemporary Black American Playwrights.* Westport, CT: Greenwood, 1988.

C62. **WELCH, LEONA N.**

C62.1. ———. *Hands in the Mirror. Center Stage.* Ed. Eileen Ostrow. Oakland: Sea Urchin Press, 1981. 268-273.

The seven-segment dramatic dance-poem pays tribute to old black women through dance.

Secondary Sources
Scholarly Criticism
Peterson, Bernard L. "Welch, Leona N." *Contemporary Black American Playwrights.* Westport, CT: Greenwood, 1988.

C63. **WILLIAMS, ANITA JANE**

C63.1. ———. *A Christmas Story. Center Stage.* Ed. Eileen Ostrow. Oakland: Sea Urchin Press, 1981. 303-309.

The one-act drama explores senility among elders. The Grandma of the drama, in her senility, steals the turkey and silverware and hides them in her room. The plot of the drama revolves around the family's attempt to retrieve the turkey and the silverware before the guests arrive for Christmas dinner.

Secondary Sources
Scholarly Criticism
Peterson, Bernard L. "Williams, Anita Jane." *Contemporary Black American Playwrights.* Westport, CT: Greenwood, 1988.

APPENDIX A: Periodicals and Journals

The following is a selected listing of magazines and periodicals that frequently publish articles on contemporary African-American female playwrights and their plays. Periodicals no longer published are marked with an asterisk (*).

African-American Review
    (Formerly *Black American*
    Literature Forum)
Afro-American
American Literature
American Theatre

Black American Literature Forum
    (Formerly *Negro American*
    Literature Forum)
Black Masks
Black Scholar
*Blackstage**
Black World (Formerly *Negro*
    Digest)*

Callalo
College Language Association
    Journal
Crisis

Drama Critique
The Drama Review

Ebony
Essense
Explicator

Freedomways

Harper's Bazaar
Helicon Nine

Jet
Journal of Dramatic Theory and
    Criticism
Journal of Ethnic Studies

Kentucky Folklore Record
The Kenyon Review

*Liberator**
Louisiana Literature

Massachusetts Review
Melus
Modern Drama
Ms.

*Negro Digest**   *Studies in American Drama*
Negro History Bulletin   *Studies in Black Literature*
The New Yorker   *Studies in the Humanities*
New York Times Magazine

                                        Theater
Partisan Review   *Theatre Journal* (Formerly
People Weekly   *Educational Theatre Journal*)
Phylon   *Theatre News*
Publisher's Weekly   *Theatre Studies*

Sage   *Variety*
Southern Exposure
Southern Quarterly   *Yale/Theatre*

APPENDIX B: About the Playwrights

The following is an alphabetical compilation of brief facts about each playwright. Where available, I have given limited biographical information for each dramatist as well as listed key works that have not been published but which have been produced. For additional biographical and play production information on selected dramatists, consult Bernard L. Peterson, Jr.'s *Contemporary Black American Playwrights and Their Plays* (*CBAP*) or James V. Hatch and Omanni Abdullah's *Black Playwrights, 1823-1977.*

ABRAMSON, DOLORES. A participant in the Sonia Sanchez Writers Workshop in 1970-71, Abramson is a poet, a short-story writer, and a playwright. Her only published drama, *The Light*, appears in Sanchez's *Three Hundred and Sixty Degrees of Blackness Comin' at You.*

AHMAD, DOROTHY. Author and playwright, Ahmad is a product of the West Coast Black Arts Movement. Her only published drama, *Papa's Daughter*, was completed in 1957, but was not produced until 1969 by the Dillard University Players in New Orleans, after being published in the Summer 1968 issue of *The Drama Review.*

ANDERSON, T. DIANNE. A playwright, TV scriptwriter, author, songwriter, theatrical technician, and teacher, Anderson was born in Buffalo, New York. Consistently active in theatre circles until she was overcome with multiple sclerosis, Anderson was a resident playwright and instructor at the Back Alley Theatre, wrote weekly scripts for the television series "Our Street," and was a visiting lecturer at the University of South Florida at Tampa.

BATSON, SUSAN. Recipient of an Obie Award for the film *AC/DC* (1971), Batson is an actress, a poet, and a playwright. Her only published drama, *Hoodoo Talkin'* appears in Sonia Sanchez's *Three Hundred and Sixty Degrees of Blackness Comin' at You*.

BEASLEY, ELOIS. A native of Chicago, Illinois, Beasley has authored several plays. In addition to her one published play, *The Fallen Angel*, she has completed *An' Long Come a Bumblebee, 1851, The Marriage* and *The Gold Shop*.

BOOKER, SUE. A TV producer, director, writer, and playwright, Booker's only published drama appears in *Cry at Birth*, edited by Merrel Booker, Sr.

BROWN, BEVERLY. Brown's one published play, *The Snake Chief*, appears in the March 1971 issue of *Negro History Bulletin*.

BROWN-GUILLORY, ELIZABETH. Playwright, scholar, and critic, Brown-Guillory in a native of Church Point, Louisiana. In addition to her regionally specific dramas, she has contributed scholarly articles to *Dictionary of Literary Biography, Phylon, SAGE*, among other places. In 1988, she published *Their Place on the Stage*, a critical examination of black women playwrights, and in 1990 she edited *Wines in the Wilderness: Plays by African American Women from the Harlem Renaissance to the Present*.

CARLOS, LAURIE. A playwright and director, Carlos is also an award-winning actress. In addition to her one published play, *White Chocolate for My Father*, her unpublished plays include *Monkey Dances, Persimmon Peel, Organdy Falsetto*, and *Nonsectarian Conversations with the Dead*.

CARROLL, VINNETTE. Actress, playwright, and artistic director of the Urban Arts Corps in New York City, Carroll is often considered one of the most outstanding black female directors in America. She received an Obie Award for acting in 1961, a Ford Foundation grant for directors, and an Emmy Award for *Beyond the Blues* (CBS 1964). In 1972, she was recognized by the Dramatists Guild Committee for Women for her contributions to the theatre, an award she shared with playwright Alice Childress.

CHARLES, MARTIE. A member of the Black Theater workshop in Harlem, Charles writes for the New Lafayette Theater Company. Her published dramas include *Job Security*, which appears in James Hatch's *Black Theater USA*, and *Black Cycle*, which appears in Woodie King and Ron Milner's *Black Drama Anthology*.

CHILDRESS, ALICE. Author, actress, playwright, director, and lecturer, Alice Childress was born in Charleston, South Carolina. She was a member of the American Negro Theatre for ten years where she acted, directed, and served as a member of the Board of Directors. In 1972, she was recognized by the Dramatists Guild Committee for Women for her contributions to the theatre, an award she shared with Vinnette Carroll. Notably, Childress is the only African American female playwright whose dramas have been written, published, and produced for over five decades.

CLARK, CHINA. A playwright, TV script writer, film writer, poet and writing teacher, Clark was born in Pennsylvania. She has taught writing for the Cell Block Theatre at Columbia University, and in 1977 she was a staff writer for the "Bill Cosby Show."

CLEAGE, PEARL. A poet, playwright, and writer, Cleage was born in Springfield, Massachusetts. In addition to her drama, she has published two volumes of poetry, *We Don't Need the Music* (1976) and *Dear Dark Faces: Portraits of People* (1980). Her fiction, other poems, and essays have also been published in *Ms.*, *Black World*, *Black Collegian*, and *Journal of Black Poetry*.

COLLINS, KATHLEEN. An associate professor of film at City College New York, Collins is a playwright, writer, film maker, director, and producer. She is the co-producer of three films—*Gouldtown: A Mulatto Settlement*, *The Cruz Brothers and Miss Mallory*, and *Losing Ground*.

COOPER, JOAN "CALIFORNIA." Short-story writer, novelist, and playwright, Cooper is known primarily as a novelist. Her one published drama, *Loners*, appears in Eileen Ostrow's *Center Stage*.

CORTHRON, KIA. Author of *Cage Rhythm*, Corthron is a member of the Dramatists Guild. Her unpublished but produced plays include *Come Down Burning*, *Catnap Allegiance*, and *Wake Up Lou Riser*.

DAVIS, THULANI. A journalist, poet, and dramatist, Davis is the author of *X*. In 1994-95, she was an artist-in-residence at the New York Shakespeare Festival.

DEVEAUX, ALEXIS. Born in New York City, DeVeaux received her Bachelor of Arts from Empire State College of SUNY in 1976. A political activist for black feminist causes, she is also a poet, playwright, fiction writer, and teacher. Her fiction includes novels *Spirit in the Street* (1973) and *Li Chen/ Second Daughter First Son* (1975), children's book *na-ni*

(1973), and a biography of blues singer Billie Holiday, *Don't Explain: A Song of Billie Holiday* (1980).

DOVE, RITA. Former poet laureate of the United States, Dove is best known for her poetry. Her lone published drama appears, in excerpt form, in the Summer 1994 issue of *Callaloo*.

FABIO, SARAH WEBSTER. Born in Nashville, Tennessee, Fabio is a playwright, poet, critic, and teacher. A prominent figure in the Black Arts Movement during the sixties, her poetry includes *A Mirror, A Soul* (1969), *Black Talk: Soul, Shield and Sword* (1973), and *Soul Ain't, Soul Is* (1973).

FLAGG, ANN (KATHRYN). A playwright and a children's theatrical director, Flagg was born in Charleston, West Virginia. She studied under noted black theatre historian Dr. Fannin S. Belcher at West Virginia State University. Her one published drama *Great Gettin' Up Morning* was published in 1964.

FRANKLIN, J.E. Born in Houston, Texas, Franklin is a playwright, an author, and a teacher. Her book *Black Girl from Genesis to Revelations* (1976) is the source for her best-known play *Black Girl*. She has published short stories and a series of articles on education through art.

FREEMAN, CAROL. A self-described, revolutionary, Black nationalist, Freeman is a poet, playwright, and short-story writer from Rayville, Louisiana. Her poetry has been anthologized in collections such as *The Magic of Black Poetry*, *The Poetry of the Negro*, and *The Poetry of Black America*. Her only published drama, *The Suicide*, was published in *Soulbook* and reprinted in *Black Fire*.

GIBSON, P.J. Author of the multiple award-winning *Long Time Since Yesterday*, Gibson is a playwright and a teacher. Born in Pittsburgh, Pennsylvania, she was educated at Keuka College in New York. In addition to her published dramas, she has completed over ten dramas that have been produced at least once.

GRANT, MICKI (MINNIE PERKINS). An actress, author, composer, and lyricist, Grant was born in Chicago, Illinois. In 1970, she became an artist-in-residence of the Urban Arts Corps in New York City, where some of her original dramatic works were written in collaboration with artistic director Vinette Carroll.

HANSBERRY, LORRAINE. A playwright, journalist, and editor, Hansberry was the first African American female to be produced on Broadway and the first African American dramatist to win the New York Drama Critics Circle Award. Her first drama, *A Raisin in the Sun* (1959), is the most frequently anthologized drama authored by an African American. Though best known for *A Raisin in the Sun,* Hansberry completed, published, and produced more than six dramatic works.

HOUSTON, DIANNE. A native of Washington, DC, Houston is an actress, director, and playwright. Her special interest in children's theatre lead her to collaborate with composer Latteta Brown to complete children's songs and a children's musical, *The Tale of Peter Rabbit: A Musical Retelling*. Her single published drama, *The Fisherman*, appears in Eileen Ostrow's Center Stage.

HUNKINS, LEE. A playwright and TV scriptwriter, Hunkins was born in New York City. In addition to her one published drama, *Revival,* Hunkins has completed and produced six other plays, two dramatic monologues, and one television play.

JACKSON, CHERRY. A philosopher and a playwright, Jackson has published one drama, *In the Master's House There Are Many Mansions* (1978), which appears in Eileen Ostrow's *Center Stage*.

JACKSON, ELAINE. An actress and a playwright, Jackson has published and produced two dramas, *Toe Jam* and *Paper Dolls*. In addition, her two-act drama *Cockfight*, directed by Woodie King, Jr., was produced at the Greenwich Mews Theatre in 1977 and ran for twenty-eight performances.

JACKSON, JUDITH ALEXA. A TV writer and performance artist, Jackson has toured the United States with her one-woman performance plays *N*gg*r*, *Huhbebah's House*, and *Origin of the Biscuit*. She has written teleplays for *The Cosby Show*, *A Different World*, *Pee Wee's Playhouse*, and *Laverne and Shirley*.

JOHNSON, CHRISTINE. A poet-playwright, Johnson has completed poetry which appears in *For Malcolm: Poems on the Life and Death of Malcolm X*. Her lone published drama, *Zwadi Ya African Kwa Dunwa* (Africa's Gift to the World), was published in 1960 by Free Black Press.

JONES, GAYL. A short-story writer, poet, novelist, critic, and playwright, Jones is a native of Lexington, Kentucky. In addition to her three dramatic works, she is the author of two novels, *Corregidora* (1975) and *Eva's*

Man (1976), a collection of short stories *White Rat* (1977), and a book of poems, *Songs for Anninho* (1981).

JONES, LOLA (LOLA JONES AMIS). A short-story writer, teacher, and playwright, Jones was born in Norfolk, Virginia. In addition to her dramatic works, she is the author of two books of short stories, *Dear Aunt & Till Fen Comes Back!* and *The Edge of Doom, or Honor Thy Father*. She is also the founding editor of the creative writers' journal *Outreach*.

KAI, NUBIA. A poet, playwright, and novelist, Kai is the recipient of the National Endowment for the Arts Award for Poetry. Her works have appeared, among other places, in *Journal of Black Poetry*, *Obsidian*, and *Black World*. Her one published play, Parting, was first produced in August 1983 by Woodie King, Jr. at the New Federal Theatre in New York.

KEIN, SYBIL. Kein's one published play, *Get Together*, appears in Elizabeth Brown-Guillory's *Wines in the Wilderness*.

KENNEDY, ADRIENNE. Born in Pittsburgh, Pennsylvania, Kennedy is a playwright and a creative writing teacher. Under the tutelage of Edward Albee, Kennedy became a recognized dramatist in theatre circles. Her best known play, *Funnyhouse of the Negro*, received a 1964 Obie Award. Since *Funnyhouse,* she has published and produced over ten dramatic works and a collection of essays, *People Who Led to My Plays* (1987).

KIMBALL, KATHLEEN. An alumna of the New York Shakespeare Festival Public Theatre, Kimball has published one drama, *Meat Rack*. In addition, *Jimtown* was produced in 1972 in New York by Theatre Genesis.

LENOIRE, ROSETTA. An actress, black theatre founder and director, and producer, LeNoire was born in New York City. In addition to her musical revue *Bubbling Brown Sugar* (1976), she has completed at least eight other unpublished dramatic works.

LINCOLN, ABBEY. A native of Chicago, Illinois, Lincoln is an actress, writer, director, playwright, and noted jazz vocalist. During the mid-1970s, she was an assistant professor of Afro-American Theatre and Pan-African Studies at California State University, and in 1975 she was elected to the Black Filmmakers Hall of Fame.

MCCAULEY, ROBBIE. An actress and a playwright, McCauley studied playwriting with the Playwrights' Workshop of the Negro Ensemble Company. In addition to her one published drama, *Sally's Rape*, she has produced two other dramatic works, *Wildflowers* and *My Father and the Wars*.

MARTIN, SHARON STOCKARD. A native of Nashville, Tennessee, Martin is a poet, playwright, theatre critic, freelance writer, and editor. Between 1978-1980, she was an associate editor of *Black Collegian* magazine as well as the communications director for the Urban League of Greater New Orleans. In addition to her two published dramas, she has completed and produced three domestic comedies, one absurdist protest comedy, and a one-act monologue.

MASON, JUDI ANN. A native of Shreveport, Louisiana, Mason was educated at Grambling State University. At age 20, she was one of the youngest women to have an Off-Broadway play produced in New York. Although she is credited with having written at least seven plays, *Livin' Fat* is her most popular published drama.

NSABE, NIA. A poet-playwright, nSabe participated in the Sonia Sanchez Writers Workshop in New York in 1970-71. Her one published drama, *Moma Don't Know What Love Is* (1971), appears in Sanchez's *Three Hundred Sixty Degrees of Blackness Comin' at You.*

O'NEAL, REGINA. An author, teacher, TV scriptwriter, broadcaster, and producer, O'Neal was born in Detroit, Michigan and educated at Wayne State University. Each of her three published plays, *Walk a Tight Rope*, *And Then the Harvest*, and *Night Watch* appears in her collection, *And Then the Harvest: Three Television Plays* (1974).

OSBORNE, PEGGY A. Osborne is the author of the one-act educational play *The Meeting* (1968), which was published by Afro-American Publishing Company.

PARKS, SUZAN-LORI. Author of *Imperceptible Mutabilities in the Third Kingdom*, Parks was the recipient of the 1990 Obie Award for Best Play. Her *Death of the Last Black Man in the Whole Entire World*, was first produced in Brooklyn in 1990 by BACA Downtown.

RAHMAN, AISHAH. A playwright and an educator, Rahman began playwriting in the sixth grade. In addition to her four published plays, Rahman has completed and produced multiple other dramatic works. Her *Lady Day*, a musical tragedy based on the life and career of Billie Holiday was directed by Paul Carter Harrison and ran for 34 performances at the Chelsea Theatre in Brooklyn.

REED, EDWINA. Reed is the author of the one-act black history play *A Man Always Keep His Word* published in the January 1963 issue of *Negro History Bulletin*.

RHODES, CRYSTAL. A playwright and a TV scriptwriter, Rhodes is a native of Indianapolis, Indiana. In 1983, she was nominated as one of the Outstanding Young Women in America. In addition to her one published drama, *The Trip* (1979), she has completed multiple dramas and she has written and co-produced numerous scripts for the television series "Getting By."

RICHARDS, BEAH.   A native of Vicksburg, Mississippi, Richards is best known for her role in *Guess Who's Coming to Dinner* (1967) as Sidney Poitier's mother. In addition to the performance piece *A Black Woman Speaks* (1950), published in Margaret Wilkerson's *Nine Plays by Black Women,* she has completed a full length showcase entitled *One in a Crowd.*

SANCHEZ, SONIA. A playwright, author, editor, revolutionary poet, and lecturer, Sanchez is a native of Birmingham, Alabama. A prolific poet of the Black Arts Movement, Sanchez has published multiple volumes of poetry, an anthology from her students in her Harlem writer's workshop, critical essays, and a children's book, *The Adventures of Fathead and Squarehead* (1974).

SHANGE, NTOZAKE. A poet, actress, dancer, musician, author, director, and educator, Shange is best known for her theatre piece *for colored girls who considered suicide/when the rainbow is enuf.* Developer of the choreopoem as a dramatic form, Shange has completed and published numerous choreopoems in addition to experimental theatre pieces like *Boogie Woogie Landscapes* and cabarets like *Where the Mississippi Meets the Amazon* (currently unpublished).

SMITH, ANNA DEAVERE. Creator and performer of her one-woman shows, Smith gained notoriety after performing *Twighlight: Los Angeles 1992: On the Road, A Search for American Character*, which chronicled the thoughts, memories, and experience of those directly affected by the riots in Los Angeles in 1992.

SMITH, JEAN WHEELER. A short-story writer and a playwright, Smith was born in Detroit, Michigan. Her one published drama, *O.C.'s Heart* appears in the April 1970 issue of *Negro Digest*.

STILES, THELMA JACKSON. Born in Monroe, Louisiana, Stiles is an author, a playwright, and an editor. Her lone published drama, *No One Woman Show*, appears in Eileen Ostrow's *Center Stage*.

TAYLOR, REGINA. Taylor's one published drama, *Mudtracks*, appears in *EST Marathon 1994: One Act Plays*.

TURNER, BETH. A playwright, actress, publisher, and teacher, Turner has completed two historical dramas, and at least three dramatic works for young audiences. Her one published play, *Crisis at Little Rock* was published in Scholastic magazine's *Search* in April 1977.

VANCE, DANITRA. Playwright and actress, Vance is the recipient of Drama-Logue Awards for her performances in *The Colored Museum* and *Spunk*. Her published essays appear, among other places, in *Genesis Journal*, *Women of Power*, and *The Choices We Made*.

WALKER, LUCY M. A playwright, theatrical director, and freelance journalist, Walker is a native of Memphis, Tennessee. Each of her seven published plays appears in her collection *Social Action in One-Act Plays* (1970).

WELCH, LEONA N. A native of Mobile, Alabama, Welch is a poet, playwright, and teacher. In addition to her one published drama, *Hands in the Mirror*, which appears in Eileen Ostrow's *Center Stage*, she has published one book of poetry, *Black Gibraltar*.

WILLIAMS, ANITA JANE. Born in Houston, Texas, Williams wrote her first play at age 16. In addition to her one published play, *A Christmas Story*, she has completed *The First Militant Protest of 42nd Street*, which was produced in the Spring of 1982 by the Black Repertory Group.

AUTHOR INDEX

The following is an alphabetical index of all authors and editors of anthologies and collections cited in Section I, of all authors and editors of books of general criticism cited in Section II, and of all playwrights cited in Section III.

SUBJECT INDEX

The following is an alphabetical index of the various subjects that are included in Section III.

TITLE INDEX

The following is an alphabetical index of titles of all anthologies and collections cited in Section I, of all books of general criticism cited in Section II, and of all plays cited in Section III.

About the Author

DANA A. WILLIAMS is a doctoral candidate at Howard University. Her current research interests include African American dramatists and novelists.

ISBN 0-313-30132-8

90000>

HARDCOVER BAR CODE